LOVE VISION

I0225062

Love Vision

Your Personal Guide to Living a Life You LOVE

Heather Lee Beasley

Copyright © 2017 **Heather Lee Beasley**
All rights reserved.

ISBN-13: **9780692838297**
ISBN-10: **0692838295**
Library of Congress Control Number: **2017901222**
Love Vision Publications, Palm Beach Gardens, FL

Contents

Introduction · ix
Glossary · xiii

Chapter 1   Black Out · 1
Chapter 2   Living in the "SSS" · · · · · · · · · · · · · · · 12
Chapter 3   Post Traumatic Stress Disorder · · · · · · 18
Chapter 4   The "SSS" Playground · · · · · · · · · · · · · 21
Chapter 5   Chronic Pain Syndrome · · · · · · · · · · · · 28
Chapter 6   The Power of Acceptance · · · · · · · · · · · 36
Chapter 7   The Power of Purpose · · · · · · · · · · · · · 45
Chapter 8   The Power of Creating Your Own RULES · · · · · 62
Chapter 9   The Power of Your Sixth Sense · · · · · · · 75
Chapter 10 Live Free or Die · · · · · · · · · · · · · · · · · 81
Chapter 11 F*CK Your Fears, Fulfill Your Destiny · · · · · 90
Chapter 12 A Student of Love · · · · · · · · · · · · · · · · 104
Chapter 13 It's Time to Ignite a "LOVE VISION" Generation! · · · · · 123
Chapter 14 Goal Training 101 · · · · · · · · · · · · · · · · 162
Chapter 15 Analogies and Symbolism · · · · · · · · · · 180
Chapter 16 Creative Visualization · · · · · · · · · · · · · 200
Chapter 17 Emotions and Feelings 101 · · · · · · · · · · 203
Chapter 18 Miracles and Manifestation · · · · · · · · · 227
Chapter 19 The Power of Gratitude · · · · · · · · · · · · 247

Chapter 20   The Power of Following Your Heart · 254

Bibliography· 275
Acknowledgments· 277
The Author · 281

Chapter Exercises

Chapter 7   Exercise: Discovering Your Purpose· 47

Mindful Exercise: "Be Where You Are" · · · · · · · · · · · · · · · · · · · 58

Chapter 8   Exercise: Creating Your Personal "Love Vision" Rules· · · · · · · · · · · 65

Chapter 9   Exercises to Access Your Intution· 77

Chapter 10   Exercise: How to Awaken Your Soul · · · · · · · · · · · · · · · · · · · 83

Exercise: Break Free from Living in Your "Comfort Zone" · · · · · · · · 86

Exercise: The Love Vision "Five W – How Question's" · · · · · · · · · · · 88

Chapter 11   Exercise: "Love Vision" Bucket List · · · · · · · · · · · · · · · · · · · 96

Chapter 12   Exercise: Self Identification- Identifying your "Authentic Truth" · · · · 114

Chapter 13   Exercise: YOLO Exercise· 134

Exercises: Writing Your VISION & Creating Your Vision Board · · · · · 156

Chapter 14   Exercise: Developing Your Personal Goals · · · · · · · · · · · · · · · · 162

Exercise: Questions for Designing an "Action Plan" · · · · · · · · · · · 174

Exercise: Building Your "Support Network" · · · · · · · · · · · · · · 177

Chapter 15   Exercise: Unleash You Inner Super Hero · · · · · · · · · · · · · · · · · · 189

Chapter 16   Exercise: How to Practice and Exercise Creative Visualization · · · · · 201

Chapter 17   Exercise: The "Channeling Method" · 209
              Exercise: Postive Affirmations · 212
              Exercise: Defining Your Presence, Passion, Preparation,
              and Perseverance ·, · · · · 224

Chapter 18   Exercise: Creating Your "Love List" · 230
              Exercise: Unleashing Your "Inner Child" · · · · · · · · · · · · · · · · · · · 237

Chapter 19   Exercise: Gratitude Journaling: 101 · 250

Chapter 20   Exercise: Heart Q & A · 256
              Exercise: Feel the Heat of Your Passion · · · · · · · · · · · · · · · · · · · 258

Introduction

WHEN I WAS twenty-three years old, I made the personal decision to undergo LASIK eye surgery to free myself from wearing glasses and contacts. In high hopes of gaining 20/20 vision, I was left beyond devastated after the surgery went wrong and I was left to live in a LASIK nightmare. Just when I thought my life was over, it was truly just beginning. God had a bigger plan. Through my personal tragedy, trials, and tribulations, I was led to the biggest transformation of my life. This one decision changed the course of my destiny. I was given a new sense of vision—"LOVE VISION."

Love Vision is an intimate story about my vision loss and how I was given a special gift: a new sense of vision that opened the eyes of my heart. I will take you on a personal journey, one in which I confront tragedy, fears, and demons after my Lasik nightmare. You will see how the power of "Love Vision" allows me to transform pain into a passion for finding restoration for my mind, body, and soul.

I will share with you the secrets, tools, and resources I discovered that enabled me to find hope, healing, and vision. *Love Vision* is more than just a book…It will take you on your own personal journey of exploration to help you face the fears that are holding you back from living your best life now. It will allow you to gain clarity on what your VISION is for your life. *Love Vision* features a built-in journal and workbook designed to help you discover your true passions and life purpose. Through powerful questioning and personal-growth exercises, you will be guided to clearly define your personal values, goals, desires, and dreams.

Love Vision is an intense mental and spiritual workout that will motivate you to connect with your mind, body, and soul. It will awaken you to your authentic truth and power so you can start taking unprecedented action toward your goals to manifest your dreams and live a life that you absolutely love. *Love Vision* will allow you to realize that you are the creator of your own life and that you're called for a higher purpose and destiny. Do not let your past define you. The past is in the past. The past is over and will never return. Your future life is waiting for you in this moment.

This is a must-read for our generation! We are living in a society that brainwashes us daily about what we must do to achieve personal success, physical beauty, power, and happiness. Our minds, belief systems, and the way in which we view the world have been polluted. We are a generation without a VISION! The message contained within *Love Vision* will touch your heart and mind; you'll realize that you're chosen for a higher calling and purpose. It will give you a new perspective that will allow you to view yourself, others, and the world from a place of love. You will begin to see your vision as a beautiful and precious gift.

You will discover how forgiveness, love, and faith can set you free from the chains of fear that are holding you back from fulfilling your dreams. Regardless of your past and current circumstances, you will learn how to harness the power of "Love Vision" so that you can fulfill your destiny. Are you ready? It's time to get your "Love Vision" on and start living a life full of passion and purpose.

The "Love Vision" Revelation

I have discovered through deep tragedy, loss, and despair that one can easily lose a sense of vision and direction in life. It is during those times that we let fear guide us on a hopeless path, where we feel as though we have no future. We must choose to turn around and take the path of love. It is love that will conquer our fears and despair. This love will give us the faith, strength, and courage that we need to continue our journeys. Love will instill in us a new vision that will enable us to live again. This vision is "Love Vision."

A Personal "Love Vision" Note to You

Dear "Love Visionary,"

I have written *Love Vision* for you. My hope is that through sharing with you my intimate story and experience of pain, tragedy, and vision loss, you will be able to directly relate it to whatever your story is. I'm going to take you on a personal journey to confront your fears, challenges, insecurities, pain, and all of the other SH*T that is holding you captive from living your best life now. My prayer is that you will be able to access your "Love Vision" and find hope, healing, and restoration.

I have included a built-in "Love Vision" journal that includes powerful questioning sections, mind-body-soul exercises, and quotes to inspire and motivate you. Just so you know, some of the questions you will be asked to answer more than once. They are the most important questions that you will ever be asked in your life, and they will help you discover what your true passions and purpose are. The only requirement that I ask as you complete the exercises is that you commit to being fully present, open hearted, honest, creative, and courageous when answering the questions. Let go of your fears, and let your heart openly answer the questions. If you need more space to write out your answers, I encourage you to use an additional notebook for your "Love Vision" journaling.

Love Vision has been specifically created to be your inspirational companion 24-7-365 days a year. The journaling and powerful questioning sections can be used at any time and virtually anywhere! The wide variety of mind-body-soul exercises that I teach will give you the opportunity to find what works best for you and your individual needs. My goal is that you will be able to utilize "Love Vision" every day. I'm sending you love, light, and freedom. You are about to begin the most exciting and fulfilling journey of your life. May your passion and purpose guide you every step of the way.

Love,

Heather Lee Beasley

Glossary

1) Love Vision- noun: the faculty or state of being able to view yourself, others, and the world from a place of love.

2) Love Visionary- noun: an individual who lives with "Love Vision" and who is committed to living their life with passion, perserverance, and purpose.

3) Love Vision Glasses- noun: the frame and lenses of love that all "Love Visionaries" wear in order to access "Love Vision."

4) Student of Love- noun: a "Love Visionary" who is grounded in their authentic truth and committed to living a life of love. One who is dedicated to being a lifelong learner of love.

5) Love Vision Generation- noun: the group of "Love Visionaries" in today's society that are living a life of love. The individuals who are the light in amidst the darkness.

6) Love Vision Rules- noun: the non-negotiable rules that all "Love Visionaries" must design for their own life, in order to fulfill their VISION. R(routines), U(You), L(live), E(everday), S(successfully and stress-free)

7) "LV" Bucket List- noun: your personal "Love Vision" bucket list of 5-10 of your biggest desires, goals, and dreams that you want to live out this year. They are strategically aligned with your VISION, passions, and purpose.

8) Love- noun: the most powerful force in the Universe. The seed of all miracles. verb: the act of unconditionally loving yourself, others, and the world.

9) "SSS"- noun: the superficial, surface, society we live in that has brainwashed most of our generation.

10) "SSS" playground-noun: the dangerous playground that our superficial, surface, society gives us. An area full of distractions and activities that assist people in having "fun" and numbing the pain in their lives.

11) "SSS" glasses-noun: the blinders that our superficial, surface, society places over our eyes so that we will become victims to their lies.

12) Fear- noun: the lies that hold you captive physically, mentally, emotionally, psychologically, and spiritually. The lies that enable you from living your best life now and fulfilling your destiny.

13) Pain- noun: the physical, mental, emotional, psychological, and spiritual anguish, sorrow, and distress that all humans experience throughout life.

14) Mind, Body, Soul- noun: the three elements that give life to all human beings and allow us to experience love.

15) Faith- noun: the ability to believe. The power that will give us direction, passion, and purpose in our daily lives.

16) Risk-verb: the act of making choices and decisions that will enable you to fulfill your goals, desires and dreams.

17) VISION- noun: the personal foundation in which you build your life. It consists of your desires, goals, and dreams. It is the driving force of your life's passion and purpose. It will enable you to fulfill your destiny.

18) Love-festation- noun: the manifestation of your dreams through the exertion of your love and intended action.

CHAPTER 1

Black Out

THERE ARE CERTAIN days, events, circumstances, and choices that change you and your life forever. February 3, 2005, was one of those days for me. I was striving to enhance my physical appearance and had made the personal decision to undergo LASIK eye surgery to free myself from wearing my glasses and contacts.

I was beyond excited about the new vision that I would gain from this twenty-minute procedure. Yes, I was nervous…very nervous. I remember sitting in the waiting room filled with others, uncertainty written all over their faces. As with any cosmetic or elective procedure, there is always a risk that something could go wrong. Thoughts raced through my head as my anxiety increased.

"Heather Beasley."

My name was announced by the young, attractive sales consultant who had been with me since my very first LASIK consultation.

I stood up and followed her to a small room, where she instructed me to take a seat and relax. She took one look into my eyes and said, "Nervous…huh?"

"Extremely," I muttered as my heart began to race faster.

"Take two of these. You'll feel much more relaxed and ready for the procedure," she calmly said, handing me two pills. After she gave me the little plastic cup filled with water, I quickly took the sedatives to calm my nerves. She then led me back to the waiting room and quietly said, "I'll be back soon to take you to the surgery room."

A few minutes later, everything seemed to be going very hazy. I started to feel extremely relaxed and less tense. As I slowly flipped through the pages in the fashion magazine that I was holding, I suddenly heard my name called to report to surgery. I stood up and followed the consultant to the surgery room.

I was briefly introduced to the surgeon who would be performing the procedure. I looked him directly in the eyes and said, "Please do your best job," as the feeling of unconsciousness overtook my body.

"Just relax. I've performed thousands of these procedures over the years. You're in good hands," he said confidently. That somewhat assured me; I had already done my research and had chosen one of the most reputable surgeons in the industry. Even famous athletes and celebrities went to this guy.

As the chair reclined backward, I meditated on the surgeon's words. He began performing the surgery on the right eye. A few minutes into the surgery, I realized something had gone wrong. I began to hear the doctor expressing concern to the medical staff that there had been a serious complication.

"We have had a complication with your right eye. Do you want us to continue the surgery on your left eye?" he asked. In that moment of my sedated unconsciousness, I murmured yes.

The two sedative pills had completely altered my state of consciousness. My mind was like Jell-O....I felt like I was in a dream. After my surgery was completed, I was led to one of the medical examining rooms. All I remember from that moment was complete and utter darkness. Everything that I could see was dark and extremely blurred. Soon I heard the voice of the consultant, who had just led my father back to the recovery room. My father entered the room and sat down beside me.

The surgeon proceeded to explain the complication that had occurred during the beginning of the surgery.

"A very rare complication has occurred. During the surgery, there was a slip. This slip in movement resulted in the unintentional cutting of the cornea on your right eye. This complication is referred to as a 'free cap.' A free corneal cap occurs when the corneal flap incision is cut all the way around the eye, so instead of leaving a hinge of attached tissue to adhere back to the patient's eye, the intended flap is a freestanding piece of tissue. In your situation, the freestanding tissue was replaced and aligned in order to adhere and heal itself back to your cornea. This is a very rare complication, and your healing process is going to be very difficult to diagnose. As for your vision, it's nearly impossible for us to predict how much of it will be restored."

I had high expectations of seeing 20/20 after surgery, so it's an understatement to say that I was devastated to have such a serious complication. The result of this complication was serious physical, mental, and emotional pain. I went to numerous medical specialists, but none could offer me a solution. My complication involved vision loss accompanied by severe nerve pain in my eyes, vision-quality defects such as ghosting (faint secondary images), reduced contrast sensitivity, night-vision disturbances, floaters, and an extremely severe and untreatable dry-eye condition. I felt very alone, depressed, and hopeless as I went from doctor to doctor and heard the same negative reports.

After endless medical appointments to some of the most respected and trusted eye specialists in the country, I still had found no hope or relief for my pain. I knew that I was going to have to be the one to find the answer to help me heal physically, mentally, and emotionally from the extreme pain that my body could no longer endure. The day that I made the decision and commitment to find healing for myself was the day that I acquired "Love Vision."

"Love Vision" is the change in your perception—physically, mentally, emotionally, intellectually, and spiritually—when you decide to view everything from a place of "Love" and not fear. Choosing to focus your mind and energy on the emotion of "Love" and not fear will completely change you and your daily life forever.

The vibrational effects of choosing "Love" will enable you to nurture, love, and care for yourself in a way that will bring healing, peace, hope, and restoration into your life. This innate "Love" that you will begin to exert on a daily basis toward yourself and others will change the course of your life. By choosing "Love" over fear, you will be granted the power to fulfill your destiny. Fear will no longer be able to hold you captive physically, mentally, emotionally, psychologically, or spiritually. Love will liberate you! Freedom, hope, peace, and massive miracles are waiting for you! It's time to change your perception. Chose "Love" over "fear," and get your "Love Vision" ON!!!!

I hope that through reading about my personal story and the new perspective that I gained from acquiring "Love Vision," you will be able to relate your own life experiences to the words that you are about to read. This book is dedicated to you and to your story. You're about to be awakened to the truth that you are the author of your own personal story and that at any given moment you can choose to change the direction of your life. Your past story does not define you and dictate your future. You have the power to change your present and future.

The Storm

Following the severe complications and pain that resulted from my Lasik nightmare, my world began to shatter. I'm sure you've heard the saying, "When it rains, it pours!" Well, I was desperately stuck in a storm, with nowhere to find shelter.

A few months after my surgery, I found out that my father was cheating on my mother. My mother made the decision to file for divorce. Shortly thereafter, my dad ended up seriously dating one of my mother's best friends. My father and I had a horrible falling out when I openly expressed to him my disapproval of his behavior and actions. I was no longer welcome to live in my parents' home, and the tension between my father and me grew.

This was the darkest period of my life. I was in such a deep state of physical, emotional, mental, and spiritual pain. I had nowhere to go. For a few weeks I crashed at a friend's house, but she was still living with her parents, so my time there quickly came to an end. My grandmother invited me stay with her because she knew that I desperately needed somewhere to go. My time spent with her was a blessing; she was a woman of great faith. Every day, she encouraged me with positive talks, scriptures, and prayers. She was and is to this day the most grounded woman in faith whom I've ever known in my life. She was determined to instill in me a renewed sense of hope and faith in God so that I would believe he still had a plan for my life. She knew the darkness and pain that I was facing, but she didn't let that deter her from speaking truth and faith into my life.

Her light ignited within me a small amount of hope. This hope became stronger when I began to pray and ask God for his direct wisdom and guidance in my life. It was through this open communication with God that I was able to develop a relationship with him. I told him everything. I was able to freely unload my pain, fears, and sorrow to him by telling him exactly how I felt. I began relying on him for strength. Each new day began to bear more light, and I became more grounded in my faith. Things started to truly change when God started to show me that he still had an incredible plan for my life. Despite all of my current circumstances, God was speaking to my soul and telling me that he was going to use my story to help others. At the time, this was hard for me to comprehend—I was desperately ashamed of the physical and emotional pain I was experiencing. How would I ever be able to open up and share my true story with others? Who was I to inspire and encourage others to have faith and hope in their lives? At the time, I didn't know how to answer these questions, but….God knew the answers, and he was planning to give me an opportunity that would change the course of my destiny.

The opportunity was a job offer in sunny South Florida. I had been praying for a sign from God and felt as though this was it. Born and raised in Pittsburgh, Pennsylvania, I dreaded the icy cold winters. From the age of five, I prayed to God, asking him if I could live in Disney World. No joke. I had always dreamed of moving to Florida! But I never imagined that I would be given the opportunity, especially during a difficult time in my life like this.

My friends and family thought I was crazy, but I said YES and moved to the Sunshine State with only a few suitcases and my 2002 Honda Civic. I knew that I desperately needed to change the course of my life. I felt as though this was a God-given opportunity that the Universe was giving me. It would take me away from my current environment, family, and friends and force me to create the changes that I so desperately needed. This would be a new chapter in my life. Was I scared? Hell yeah! But I knew deep in my heart that God was calling me there and that this was part of his plan. I can't even explain it to you…but deep in my heart…I knew that I had to go. So I said YES! It was that simple. I said yes to the Universe. I began packing my suitcases with all of the summer clothes that I owned. Little did I know that it would be in the Sunshine State where the lightness would overtake my life.

This was a huge leap of faith for me, since I knew no one in Florida. I clearly remember saying good-bye to my family and friends on the day that I left Pittsburgh. I was leaving everything that I had ever known behind. It's very strange though, even though I was scared sh*tless, I didn't let fear control me. There was this energy of love, faith, and hope that started to rise up in my soul. It's hard to explain, but I can distinctly recall the feeling that I had sitting in the airplane as it took off. It was a feeling that I never experienced before. Even though I was at one of the most difficult times in my life, I began to feel a supernatural power come over my mind, body, and soul. This undeniable energy began shifting my energy. As the plane ascended into the air, I felt as though my new life was about to begin. It was a plane ride that I will never forget. I had so many questions that were racing through my mind. How long would I live in Florida? Would my job work out? Would I be able to financially support myself to live on my own? How much am I going to miss my family and friends? Will I be able to make new friends and build a life for myself? Will I even like the area that I'm moving to? Am I making a huge mistake? Will I be able to do this all on my own? All of these questions kept racing in my mind. During that flight, I had an epiphany. I realized that there was no way I could predict my future, and that I would have to live in order to answer those questions. The feelings of being scared started to dissipate in the air. I was ready to start a new beginning, regardless of what unfolded. When the plane landed, I was excited to see my new surroundings in Jupiter, Florida. This would soon become my home.

From the moment that I arrived at the Palm Beach International Airport, the Universe began placing the appropriate people, circumstances, situations, jobs, opportunities, and resources into my life. Each one directed me a step closer to fulfilling my destiny. The first few months of settling into my new environment, were jam-packed with activities and responsibilities with my job. One day, my job required me to venture out into the community in order to complete some necessary errands. Since I didn't know the area that well, I was relying on my GPS to guide me to my destination. Unfortunately, I got lost. I had no idea where I was. So, what's a girl to do? I saw a Wendy's Restaurant on the side of the road and I pulled over. I figured that Wendy's was a pretty safe place and that I could ask one of the locals for directions. Once I got inside, I first needed to use the restroom before I asked anyone for directions. When I entered the bathroom, there was a young girl around my age standing at the sink washing her hands. I quickly said hello and then told her that I was lost, being that I just moved to the area and didn't know my way around. She looked at me and smiled and began to laugh.

She said, "You're never going to believe this...but I'm locked out of my apartment. I can't find my key and my roommate is still at work, so I figured that I would come here to kill some time." In that awkward moment, we both began to laugh. After leaving the restroom, we continued chatting. Her name was Jenny, she was super-sweet, funny, and smart. She said to me, "Since we are here, would you like to get something to eat?" I laughed and said "That would be great, as I'm really hungry." So we ended up grabbing a bite to eat and ended up talking for over an hour. We both shared where we were from, the colleges we attended, and how we both ended up in Florida. Jenny was new to the area as well, as she moved with her roommate from North Carolina for a new job and to live closer to the beach. We both were in similar uncharted territories.

Getting ready to leave, she said "This may sound kind of strange, but do you want to exchange phone numbers? Since you don't really know anyone here, maybe we could hang out sometime and I could introduce you to some of my friends." I smiled and said "I would love that. I really enjoyed talking with you." So, we exchanged phone numbers. The rest is history. Jenny and her friends ended up becoming my best friends and Florida family. I will never forget the memories, laughs, crazy times, and challenges that we all shared. Together, we experienced living our lives' to the fullest in our twenty's. I truly believe to this day that meeting Jenny in the bathroom at Wendy's was a divine appointment.

Shortly after meeting Jenny and her friends, I ended up winning a contest on the radio. I called when I heard the call to action on my favorite radio station in order to win tickets for a VIP event in West Palm Beach. I was so excited when I found out that I won! I'd be able to take my new friends to the one of the biggest events in the city! We had a blast! That night I ended up meeting a few people who worked for the radio station. Little did I know that I would end up working with them. A few weeks after the event, I was in my car driving and listening to the radio station that I had won the contest from. A commercial came on that announced that the company was hiring new Account Executives for their Sales and Marketing team. I was very intrigued. This sounded like something that I would really enjoy doing. I felt as though this could be a great opportunity! They were holding an upcoming career fair in the city, so I decided to go. While I was there, I was able to reconnect with the people who worked for the radio station, that I had met at the VIP event a few weeks earlier. I was able to find out more details of the job position that was available, and I even scheduled an interview. The interview went great and I ended up getting the job! I was working for one of the top broadcasting companies in the country!

My job as an Account Executive was to sell radio space and to help write the commercials for clients. I find it very ironic that I ended up working in this role. You may be wondering why I said this. The reason that I believe it to be so ironic, is because the first time that I heard about LASIK eye surgery was from a radio commercial. Prior to making the decision to get LASIK, I kept hearing a testimonial radio commercial that was hosted by a very famous athlete. I swear I must have heard the commercial at least fifty times. The endorser raved about his experience and the freedom that he gained from the short and painless procedure. The repetitive message and call to action that I heard, impacted me. I felt as though I needed to have this procedure. I ended up responding to this call to action. When reflecting back to my time as an Account Executive, I see it as a blessing. I was given a rare opportunity to learn the media industry inside out. I learned how the media crafts call-to-action messages that tell people what they need to do, buy, have, maintain, and achieve in order to be happy. I also learned a lot about how advertising and marketing directly impacts our society. All of this information that I gained, would later help me to fulfill my purpose.

Over the past thirteen years, I have been blessed with amazing opportunities that allowed me to build an extremely successful career in sales and marketing. I have been able to work for some of the most successful and well-known companies in their respective industries. Through these various work experiences, I have been able to learn more about myself and my interests, passions, gifts, and the talents that God has given me.

By attending a women's success seminar in Miami, I discovered life coaching. This seminar changed the course of my life. It was at this event, where hundreds of women gathered to be inspired and encouraged, that my heart finally found its true calling.

This new career path was calling me. It was speaking to my heart. I knew that I had to say yes! Deep inside, I knew that this was what God was calling me to do and that this was part of his master plan for my life. In choosing to become a life-coach, I was then able to answer the questions that I asked myself right before my move to Florida. These were the questions that I now could finally answer: How would I ever be able to open up and share my true story with others? Who was I to inspire and encourage people to have faith and hope in their lives, in others, and in the Universe?

Now, answering those questions is easy, for I know who I am and what I'm called to do in my life. I am called to share my message of "Love Vision" with you so that you can ignite the faith, hope, and passion in your life and be set free from fear. Sometimes you just need to say "YES" even if you're scared to death and know that your decision is risky. Risks reap rewards! Say "YES" to you, your goals, and your dreams! Saying "YES" will change the course of your life.

What Is "Love Vision"?

Through my own personal experience of enduring "vision loss" and extreme physical pain, I was enlightened to find healing through accessing a new type of vision. It was at my darkest moment of hopelessness, pain, and despair that "Love Vision" fell upon me. Although it was but one glimmer of light, this light contained enough "Love" to cast out the hopelessness and darkness that I could no longer live in. It was at this moment that my life really changed—forever.

It was a miraculous moment in which I believe a power much greater than myself, opened the eyes of my heart. At that moment I realized that "Love" was the only hope that I had left and that my life was worth living. It was this epiphany that awakened me and ignited me with the power to access my "Love Vision." For this new vision opened my mind, body, and soul to a whole new perspective that enabled me to view and live my life with love.

This perspective changed my destiny and gives me the strength every day to live a life that I love. We are all called to live a life we love. But we must have a VISION for our lives, and that VISION must be full of love.

Love Vision was written with the sole purpose of inspiring you to open the eyes of your heart, mind, and soul in order to live the life that you were destined. It is my goal to become your personal one-on-one life coach as you read *Love Vision*. I will walk beside you as you confront your biggest fears, challenges, struggles, and demons in order to gain freedom and reclaim your power. Step-by-step, I will guide you to gain clarity on your desires, goals, and dreams so that you can create a VISION that will enable you to fulfill your destiny. I will help you to create a strategy and plan that will that will contain the steps you need to take on a daily basis to start living a life you love.

I will share with you the powerful steps, visualization techniques, and exercises that I used to transform my physical pain into a passion to change my life—physically, emotionally, psychologically, and spiritually. You will be guided to authentically connect to your mind, body, and soul in order to get your "Love Vison" ON—or should I say, "OM"! This new vision that you're about to access will drastically transform your perception of yourself, your life, others, and your ability to live in a way that you have never even imagined. This is the beginning of healing.

Are you ready to live a life full of passion, inspiration, courage, faith, and strength? Then turn the page; you are about to be awakened to the truth that our generation has been too long awaiting. You're chosen.

Prepare to dig deep within yourself to access your innermost passions, strengths, and internal resources. You must be ready to discover the fears and limiting belief—systems that have been deceiving, cheating, and holding you back for years from fulfilling your true destiny and calling. "Love Vision" will reveal to you that you're "chosen" and will instill a faith in you that you have the power to accomplish anything that you put your heart and soul into.

CHAPTER 2

Living in the "SSS"

WE ARE ALL human beings...We are all one. We are all souls living in human physical bodies. We are wonders of the upmost creator of this Universe....a miraculous creation of being. We are physical, emotional, spiritual, and psychological beings who feel and perceive each and every moment of our existence. We are living in a society that is consumed with viewing things from a very superficial, surface level.

This superficial society is what I like to refer to as the "SSS" (superficial-surface society). The "SSS" has successfully brainwashed most of our generation and has told us infinite lies in hopes of altering our belief system. The "SSS" lies to us on a daily basis and tells us that we are not good enough, attractive enough, successful enough, smart enough, or capable of achieving what we desire unless we "BLANK."

The "BLANK SPACE" is the "what" that society is trying to sell us....materialistically, socially, or culturally speaking. Use your imagination and fill in the "BLANK SPACE" with the what your mind-set and belief system have bought into or have been at least been exposed to.

The media is greatly responsible for a lot of these false messages and utterly deceiving lies. Television, the Internet, radio, magazines, movies, social media, etc....are all constantly fixed on sending out specific messages as to "what" you need to buy or alter about yourself physically to increase your worth and happiness. These messages are very direct in trying to alter and dilute your mind and belief system to make you feel as if you need what they're selling you. These "things" that the "SSS" is constantly trying to sell us have in turn greatly and negatively affected our society and generation.

Most of us wear very dark-colored and foggy glasses that the media has given to us to help us see and view the world from its perspective. The lenses on these glasses project a materialistic, egocentric, and surface perspective that will help the media sell a product, service, cosmetic procedure, idea, and so on.

As a result, our inherent belief systems, mind-sets, and perceptions of ourselves and the world have been negatively affected and changed. It sounds crazy, but as you start to really think about it...you will start realizing how much truth is in this revelation.

The "SSS" is after all of our society. A great example of this is the many beautiful and successful people in the entertainment business, such as celebrities, models, and musicians. They're considered some of the most beautiful people in the world, people who "have it all." Many of our youth today even idolize these individuals, aspiring to be more like them.

The "SSS" shines a light on these successful individuals, which gives them a very intoxicating and alluring appeal. The spotlight that shines so brightly on these individuals casts a very powerful glare on our already foggy and dirty lenses in which we view the world. Ironically, even the famous and rich are affected. As we see in many of the *True Hollywood Story* documentaries of celebrity's lives, things aren't always as they appear. No matter who you are; what you do for a living; or who your family, friends, or lover are—we all are searching.

Since many of us have been "brainwashed" into believing these lies from society, our belief systems have been drastically altered. From birth we all have lived, experienced, and felt great pain. This pain for all of us has been physical, emotional, spiritual, and psychological. The "SSS" has lied to us and has offered up a variety of solutions for "numbing" this pain. The temporary fixes and so-called solutions that we have turned to include drugs, alcohol, sex, abuse, money, food, bad relationships, a mission to achieve unrealistic "perfection," and unhealthy habits that all lead to very dangerous and life-threatening outcomes.

The "SSS" has steered our generation on a purposeless, unfulfilling, and dangerous journey. This path leads us on a daily search to fill the void and numb the pain in the moment…in hopes that we will dilute our own pain. Sadly, this tumultuous and unfulfilling path has only resulted in increased and deeper levels of pain physically, emotionally, spiritually, and psychologically.

The moment you become fully aware that we are all living in the "SSS," you will awaken. We are living in a society that perceives and focuses mostly on the physical of human beings. This society prefers to close its eyes to the emotional, mental, spiritual, and psychological realms of our physical, human existence. It's now time for our generation to wake up and take off those dark-colored and foggy lenses that the "SSS" has placed over our eyes and put on our "Love Vision"! It's time to get our "Love Vision" ON and ignite a radical change and movement in our society.

Many of us have endured different types of pain due to the personal experiences of our own individual lives. Some of us have had very tough and difficulty journeys. For many, there are days when one does not even want to go on due to lack of hope. I've been there…I didn't think that I was going to make it. But I'm here to tell you…that there is hope. There is a reservoir that is waiting for you…This reservoir is springing forth of hope, belief, faith, strength and love. It's time we "wake up" our society and ignite the "LOVE VISION GENERATION."

A Symbolic Dream

As I began to write this book and express my innermost thoughts, beliefs, values, and life experiences, a very tumultuous emotional storm started brewing in my soul. I began "feeling" on a different emotional and psychological level. This new "feeling" that I began experiencing is hard to accurately describe. This emotional level enabled me to start "feeling" and truly assessing the emotions of others. Overwhelmed by this new perception, I had a very disturbing and symbolic dream. This dream was unlike any dream that I've ever had in my entire life. It left a marked impression on my soul.

I will do my best to accurately describe to you the details of this dream, as it seemed very real to me.

The chill in the night air was evident. There was a very alarming crime scene developing on the highway interstate in the big city. All traffic was delayed, the result of a very bad car collision. Police officers were scattered everywhere. The officers were pacing the scene with flashlights in hand, searching for the criminals whom were to blame for the accident. You're probably curious as to what suspicious and illegal activities these so-called "criminals" had committed. The criminals were to blame for the multi-car collision on the highway. The reason for this collision is that the criminals were "jewel thieves" who were on an escape route and had collided with innocent drivers.

Destroyed vehicles were sprawled across the roadways. The criminals were actually driving an ambulance. All of the ambulance doors were flung wide open; the most beautiful and captivating jewels were stored in the cabin.

The ambulance was not the only place these jewels were located. The severe crash and impact on the ambulance during the collision had caused the jewels to be dispelled for miles along the interstate.

This life-threatening accident involved not only the lives of the innocent drivers and passengers but also the lives of the others who observed the crime. After mentally processing the initial shock of the horrifying situation, people began to notice the beauty of the brightly shining jewels. The allure and appeal of these jewels captivated the victims and observers. Upon realizing that these precious jewels were available at their disposal, many began to hurry and steal the jewels for themselves.

It was as though a hypnotic power had overtaken many of the innocent bystanders and victims, who disregarded the danger of the scene. Ignorance, greed, and lust for the jewels overtook the hearts of these individuals. As they scurried to gather more of the brightly colored gems, the criminals raced to take these individuals hostage. All the innocent people that were kidnapped by the criminals were bound in gold chains. The criminals succeeded in their goal of escaping the police officers and taking ransom. They escaped with their newly found victims to a nearby hospital.

I was captured in this horrifying dream. I was held hostage and bound in beautiful gold chains. Surrounding me were chained prisoners who I didn't know and couldn't communicate with. The remainder of the dream was filled with the most horrifying emotional, mental, and psychological pain that I have ever physically experienced. This dream was the worst nightmare that I had ever had in my life! For weeks I continued to replay the dream over in my mind, searching for some significance and meaning. The more I began reflecting on this haunting dream, more vivid memories began to surface.

I began to remember that there were many onlookers who had been able to escape the criminals. The ones who escaped were "awakened" and fully aware of the danger of the crime scene. These alert individuals were extremely diligent in escaping to safety and freedom.

Images began to flash before my eyes of the onlookers who were caught up in the confusion of the greed and lust that overtook their senses. The captives who fell under this dark and evil spell were held as prisoners for eternity. I was one of them. The mental, emotional, and psychological pain that we endured was eternal anguish. Although we were bound in gold chains and surrounded by the most beautiful jewels in the world, we were cut off completely from our world and those whom we loved. Our souls were tormented. We soon began to lose all faith and hope that we would ever find true freedom and be rescued.

As the dark details and emotional pain of this dream started surfacing, the significance and symbolism soon became very clear to me. The criminals in this dream were the "SSS," strategically using their beautiful and alluring jewels to captivate the minds and souls of many. They came to steal, kill, and destroy. Let this dream serve as a wake-up call for our generation. We need to "awaken" and reclaim our freedom. This freedom is love. The truth will set us free. Love is the answer.

CHAPTER 3

Post Traumatic Stress Disorder

SHORTLY AFTER MY severe LASIK complication, I was diagnosed with post-traumatic stress disorder (PTSD). The name is pretty self-explanatory, although to further educate yourself on this serious condition, please take a moment to read the brief overview of information that I obtained from the Mayo Clinic website.

"PTSD is a mental health condition triggered by a terrifying event. This can include either experiencing the event or witnessing it. Symptoms may include flashbacks, nightmares, severe anxiety, as well as uncontrollable thoughts about the event. Many people who go through traumatic events have difficulty adjusting and coping for a while. But with time and taking care of oneself, such traumatic reactions usually get better.

In some cases, the symptoms can get worse and last for months or even years. Sometimes these symptoms completely shake up a person's life. In a case such as this, it is very likely that the person will develop PTSD. Getting treatment as soon as possible after symptoms develop may prevent long-term PTSD.

A person can develop PTSD when they go through, see, or learn about an event that causes intense fear, helplessness, or horror. Doctors aren't always sure why some people have the condition. People of all ages can develop PTSD. Although, there are certain risk factors that may make you more likely to develop PTSD after a traumatic event. These include the following: being female, having experienced other trauma earlier in life, having other mental health problems, such as anxiety or depression, lacking a good support system of family and friends, having first-degree relatives with mental health problems, including PTSD; and having been abused or neglected as a child.

Women may be at increased risk of PTSD because they are more likely to experience the kinds of trauma that can trigger the condition.

There are a number of traumatic events that can lead to post-traumatic stress disorder, including: fire, natural disaster, mugging, robbery, assault, civil conflict, car accident, plane crash, torture, kidnapping, life-threatening medical diagnosis, terrorist attack and other extreme or life-threatening events. PTSD is especially common among those who have served in combat. It's sometimes called "shell shock," "battle fatigue," or "combat stress." The most common events leading to the development of PTSD include the following: combat exposure, rape, childhood neglect and physical abuse, sexual molestation, physical attack, and being threatened with a weapon.

Post-traumatic stress disorder can disrupt a person's entire life: their job, relationships, and even their enjoyment of everyday activities. Having PTSD also may place an individual at a higher risk of developing other mental health problems, including: depression, drug abuse, alcohol abuse, eating disorders, and suicidal thoughts and actions."

After reading the synopsis of PTSD, you're now aware of this serious disorder and the negative power that it holds on many people's lives. At any moment while you were reading this overview, did you once pause and contemplate its significance to your own personal experiences and life? PTSD can develop when one goes through, sees, or learns about an event that causes intense fear, helplessness, and horror. Living in our "SSS," we are constantly exposed to such events, circumstances, and environments.

In a sense, we are all suffering. I'm not saying that we all have PTSD. It's just that I believe the emotional and psychological pain we have experienced over the years has not been properly addressed. We continue to ignore the internal trauma, hoping it will dissipate. We are on a continual search to numb our pain with alcohol, sex, drugs, money, material possessions, popularity, status, food, bad relationships, a mission to achieve unrealistic "perfection," and all of our other unhealthy habits that ultimately lead us on a downward spiral.

These extremely negative coping mechanisms produce serious complications in our personal lives. Our emotional, physical, psychological, and even spiritual states of being are disrupted as a result. This ultimately breaks the mind, body, and soul connection that we need to maintain in order to live healthy, happy, and prosperous lives. Our generation is in desperate need of a specialized treatment that will help us regain the "mind-body-soul connection" to ourselves, each other, and our world at large. This alternative therapy is "Love Vision."

CHAPTER 4

The "SSS" Playground

WE ALL CAN remember the hours we loved spending on the playground as children. When we were there, it was as though life completely froze still, and all we had was "fun." We would anxiously await the school bell to ring for recess. The moment the alarm would sound, we would race out of the classroom to our place of freedom and fun. There was the swing set, sliding board, monkey bars, and sandbox. This is where all the action happened.

Fast forward to today's time...and we come to the realization that we still have a playground we frequently visit. But this is the "SSS" playground, and it offers its visitors a large variety of attractions and activities that will assist them in having "fun" and numbing the pain in their lives. This "SSS" playground is unlike the one you enjoyed while you were a child. This playground is dangerous. It has the potential to kill you mentally, emotionally, spiritually, and even physically. The "SSS" playground offers the most alluring and mesmerizing outlets for "fun." This is the place that we so often go and can never leave. We become addicted to the "fun" we have on this amusing playground. This place offers us temporary pain relief. When we are there and partaking in the various adventures and activities, we feel a sense of freedom. However, this "high" and feeling of elation will only last for a fleeting moment. As time passes, so do the feelings that the vices offered you. We are then left alone with ourselves, feeling even emptier and unfulfilled inside. This begins a process of seeking "SSS" fun to fill the void in our lives.

We continue playing on this playground with the underlying intent to find pain relief and peace in our lives. This leads us on a dangerous spiral of self-destruction. The "fun" overtakes our lives and holds us back from living our true destiny and calling. We become victims of the "SSS." We are now held captive on the "SSS" playground and wear daily the "SSS" glasses (blinders).

All we now can see are the superficial and surface surroundings of our environments. We become completely blind to the mental, emotional, and spiritual world that exists outside of the playground. For those who are held hostage and living on the "SSS" playground, they will never be able to grow up. They will be just like children who never want to leave the playground.

Their gifts, talents, and strengths will never have the opportunity to grow and flourish. They will spend their lives focused on meaningless "fun" activities. Time will quickly pass, and they will have no fruits of their labor. They will be mentally, emotionally, and spiritually unfulfilled, numb, and empty. It's time to get our "Love Vision" on and exit the playground. For we have a higher destiny and calling to fulfill.

Exiting the Playground

The Exit to Recovery, Freedom, and Purpose

The first step we must take when we decide to exit the playground is to put on our "Love Vision" glasses. We are now leaving a place that was of extreme comfort and fulfillment to our physical bodies, and we must choose to view the road ahead with love. We are about to enter into a whole new earth. This earth contains unlimited opportunities and possibilities. It is a place where we can find true love, peace, happiness, and hope.

We now are aware that we have a choice to view the world externally and internally with love as opposed to fear. Through this empowering knowledge, we will be able to touch the lives of many. "Love Vision" will be the catalyst that will enable us to release our deepest pains, fears, sorrows, and regrets. Its power will enlighten us to access the faith, peace, love, strength, and courage that reside inside of ourselves. A reservoir of hope will begin to spring forth in our hearts. Through acts of love, kindness, generosity, care, and encouragement to others, our world will greatly begin to change. People's lives will be changed forever. We will change.

"Love Vision" will bring about a drastic perception change in our lives. Our thoughts, beliefs, and feelings will slowly begin to reshape, forming our new reality. This new reality that we are about to enter into is the VISION that we have for our lives. Now that we have exited the playground and have made the decision to grow, we must have a precise and detailed vision for our lives. This vision will serve as our master plan. It will be composed of the necessary actions, choices, and goals that we need to complete in order to fulfill our vison. This vision that we create for ourselves will shape our future and destiny. It will greatly impact our today, tomorrow, and eternity. Your VISION is your legacy.

Growing Pains

Warning!!! This serves as an important advisory warning to all new "Love Visionaries" who just left the playground. This message is to inform you that your new lifestyle change is about to provoke an extensive and significant period of growing pains. Don't worry, panic, or freak out! It's actually quite normal to endure growing pains when you first start utilizing your "Love Vision."

The experience of letting go and disposing of your familiar, comfortable, yet extremely toxic behaviors, beliefs, thoughts, and actions is extremely painful. Suffering withdrawal symptoms is to be expected. This is very serious business we are talking about here! You have just made the decision to embark on a life-altering process of acknowledging and releasing all of your harmful and toxic habits, thoughts, beliefs, and actions. You now are fully aware of the necessary changes that you need to make in order to change the course of your life. This is not easy. In reality, it is one of the most challenging and difficult tasks that you will ever choose to undertake.

It's very likely that you will begin to strongly question the significance, importance, and underlying effectiveness of "Love Vision." During this painful transition period of the disposal of your former negative ways, you will begin to feel as though all of your biggest temptations, toxic addictions, and harmful desires surround you. It will begin to feel as though seductive spirits are lurking around you, tormenting and tempting you with the thoughts and desires of your old life. The life that was easy, fun, and extremely fulfilling in the "moment."

This new "Love Vision" that you were so excited about will start to seem less attractive and appealing once the realization sets in that this is a drastic lifestyle change. This is when your dedication to the decision to live a life of "Love Vision" will be tested. You must be prepared to pass this test. You must prepare yourself with courage, inspiration, motivation, faithfulness, hope, and love in order to pass this test and all future tests that you are faced with. For in passing these tests, you will be granted the experience, wisdom, and strength to build, live, and fulfill your ultimate destiny.

Turning Your Back on Fear

I've had a very strong desire since my surgery to write about how the transformative power of pain changed my life, passion, and purpose. I never had the courage to begin even typing one sentence—because of fear. You might ask, fear of what? Fear of admitting the truth. Fear is absolutely horrified at the revelation of truth. Why? Because fear is the opposite of truth. Fear is a lie. Fear is what holds us captive, imprisoned, and living in chains. These chains hold us so fiercely that we are unable to move and live our lives.

We need to be honest with ourselves, others, and our world and reveal the truth. The truth will set us free. Be prepared to dig deep within yourself, and search your soul. You need to discover your authentic truth. You need to own, share, and live your truth with the world. Do not conform to the lies of fear. You are chosen to overcome pain and fear. We must choose love and courage.

Tragedy + Trials + Tribulation = Transformation

It is in our darkest moments of despair that we realize we desperately need the light. The tragedy, trials, and tribulations that we encounter in our lives can paralyze us and allow us to choose fear to rule our lives. When we allow fear to overtake our minds, bodies, and souls, we are choosing to adopt the "SSS blinders," and we completely lose sight of our destined birthright to live a life of love.

This fear begins to dominate our thoughts, mind-sets, and beliefs about ourselves, others, and the world. When we choose to live in fear, we are choosing to live in darkness. In this darkness, we are tormented daily by our demons, who brainwash us to believe that we have no hope and future. These demons play on our insecurities, doubts, and fears. Their main job is to continually nurture our fears with the lies that they continually feed us. Our minds, bodies, and souls quickly become very unhealthy; we are existing on a lie-and-fear-based diet. We become victimized to these demons and allow them to take control over our lives.

There is hope. Your personal tragedy, trials, and tribulations can lead you to the most amazing transformation in your life. For when you are in your depths of darkness, you can choose to let the light in. You have the choice to reclaim your birthright to live a life of love. You must choose to face your demons and tell them that they have no control over your mind, body, and soul. You need to allow yourself to embrace the darkness and the truth of your tragedy, trials, and tribulations. When you fully embrace this, you will gain a new sense of strength that will allow you to cast out all of the fear, demons, and darkness in your life. When you detox yourself of fear, there will be a great void of empty space. You must immediately replace this space with Love, Faith, and Hope. This powerful combination is what I refer to as the "Transformation Trio"!

The "Transformation Trio" of "Love, Faith, and Hope" will ignite a spark in your life… that will begin to shine and start to cast out the darkness. At first, you may only see a glimmer of light as your mind, body, and soul begin to take off your "SSS blinders" of fear. You must make the conscious decision to live the "Transformation Trio" of "Love, Faith, and Hope" daily. If you do this, every day…you will become stronger, and your light will continue to glow brighter. Its flame will begin to spread to cast out all the darkness from your life so that you can live a life of freedom.

Words of Wisdom on Tragedy, Trials, and Tribulations

Grief does not change you, it reveals you.

—JOHN GREEN

Anything you lose comes round in another form.

—RUMI

It is worth remembering that the time of greatest gain in terms of wisdom and inner strength is often that of greatest difficulty.

—DALAI LAMA

Grief is a normal and natural response to loss. Keeping grief inside increases your pain.

—Anne Grant

The most beautiful people I've known are those who have known trials, have known struggles, have known loss, and have found their way out of the depths.

—Elisabeth Kubler-Ross

There is a sacredness in tears. They are not the mark of weakness, but of power. They speak more eloquently than ten thousand tongues. They are the messengers of overwhelming grief, of deep contrition, and of unspeakable love.

—Washington Irving

Make the most of your regrets: Never smother your sorrow, but tend and cherish it 'til it comes to have a separate and integral interest. To regret deeply is to live afresh.

—Henry David Thoreau

When our days become dreary with low-hovering clouds of despair, and when our nights become darker than a thousand midnights, let us remember that there is a creative force in this universe, working to pull down the gigantic mountains of evil, a power that is able to make a way out of no way and transform dark yesterdays into bright tomorrows.

—Martin Luther King Jr.

CHAPTER 5

Chronic Pain Syndrome

THROUGHOUT MY PERSONAL journey of finding help and healing for my nerve pain, I never gave up. I came very close…..many times, but I kept fighting to find healing. I'll never forget the day that a particular physician diagnosed me with chronic pain syndrome. The following diagnosis dramatically transformed my mission to find relief.

"You're experiencing something very real," my physician said. "The complication of your LASIK surgery has resulted in severe nerve pain. Your optic nerves have been severed, and you feel that pain. This painful condition is what we refer to as chronic pain syndrome. You need to read about this condition and accept it."

His words struck me like lightning. My entire body froze. It was at that moment that I fully became awakened to the truth that I needed to accept my pain in order to overcome it.

After leaving the doctor's office that day, I began researching chronic pain syndrome (CPS). The following is a medical description of CPS that I came across while searching the Internet:

Chronic Pain Syndrome (CPS) is a common problem that presents a major challenge to health-care providers because of its complex natural history, unclear etiology, and poor response to therapy. CPS is a poorly defined condition. CPS is a constellation of syndromes that usually do not respond to the medical model of care. This condition is managed best with a multidisciplinary approach, requiring good integration and knowledge of multiple organ systems. Management of chronic pain in patients with multiple problems is complex, usually requiring specific treatment, simultaneous psychological treatment, and physical therapy. Treatment of chronic pain syndrome (CPS) must be tailored for each individual patient. The treatment should be aimed at interruption of reinforcement of the pain behavior and modulation of the pain response. The goals of treatment must be realistic and should be focused on restoration of normal function (minimal disability), better quality of life, reduction of use of medication, and prevention of relapse of chronic symptoms. (Manish K Singh)

After reviewing this article, I began researching everything that I could find on CPS. I slowly started to feel empowered as I armed myself with the knowledge of this condition. The more I began to understand it, the more I realized that I needed to accept my condition in order to live my best life now. It took me too many years of living in pain, depression, and fear to come to this powerful realization. The moment when I fully accepted my condition was the moment I found a true sense of relief and experienced a revelation. I started to view the world in a whole new light. I began to realize that we are all truly connected in this world and that we all are suffering from CPS. This revelation is now yours. You're now being awakened to the secret wisdom that has been kept hidden from our generation.

As long as we are living human beings, we will always be exposed and susceptible to physical, emotional, psychological, and spiritual pain during our existence on this earth. That is part of human nature. We have all endured great and varying levels of pain due to sickness, disease, sadness, abuse, depression, abandonment, deception, anger, bad relationships, resentment, and emotional and physical trauma. The list of pain sources is endless. But, wait…there is good news. There is hope. We can move forward and live lives full of faith, freedom, and strength. The choice is yours. Yes, it is a personal choice that you must make daily. No one else can make this choice for you. You must wake up every day and make the decision to accept and release your pain and fears. If you awaken yourself to this truth and commit daily to releasing your pain and fears, you will be able to release its toxic powers on your life.

We have two options. We can either live in pain daily or choose to accept what we feel, confront it, and then release it. Freedom is here. Accept and release it, baby!

Overcoming the Power of Pain and Fear

For many years I struggled with learning how to cope with PTSD and CPS on a daily basis. I will be completely honest with you and admit that there were many times when I just wanted to give up. However, it was my passion to find healing that kept me moving forward. I visited countless pain doctors, searching for relief for my physical pain. I tried numerous medications, although my body could not handle the side effects. I read every pain and self-help book that I could in hopes of finding a solution for relief.

I was on a mission to live a better life. At many points during my search for pain relief, I became extremely depressed. I could no longer handle the physical, emotional, and psychological pain that resided in my body. I was at my breaking point when I fully accepted the reality of my pain. I was ready to explore alternative therapies to help me release it.

I remember reading an article on how acupuncture may be helpful in improving symptoms of both CPS and PTSD. Although I get faint at even the thought of a needle, I summoned up the courage to google local acupuncturists. I soon came across the website of a very well-known local acupuncturist. After reviewing his credentials and experience, I called and booked the initial consultation.

I will admit, I was extremely skeptical and actually quite scared of the first consultation that I scheduled with the acupuncturist. Thankfully, my strong desire and motivation to release my pain from CPS overrode my fears and gave me the courage to show up to my appointment.

You're probably reading this right now and thinking exactly the same thing that I was as I anxiously sat waiting in the acupuncturist office: "NEEDLES, NEEDLES, NEEDLES!!!!" For those of you who don't know exactly what acupuncture is, let me explain.

Mayo Clinic explains it quite simply, stating the following:

> Acupuncture involves the insertion of extremely thin needles through your skin at strategic points on your body. A key component of Traditional Chinese medicine, acupuncture is most commonly used to treat pain. Traditional Chinese medicine explains acupuncture as a technique for balancing the flow of energy or life force—known as qi or chi (CHEE)—believed to flow through pathways (meridians) in your body. By inserting needles into specific points along these meridians, acupuncture practitioners believe that your energy flow will re-balance. There also is evidence that acupuncture works best in people who expect it to work. Since acupuncture has few side effects, it may be worth a try if you're having trouble controlling pain with more-conventional methods.

So now you have the down low on exactly what acupuncture is and what I was about to experience for the first time. As I followed the doctor back to the "needle" room, my heart began to race. He directed me to take a seat on the chair adjacent to the window. An overwhelming peace quickly overcame my entire body as the kind physician began to ask me numerous questions about my condition and why I chose to book the initial consultation. He listened intently and nodded as I gave him the details of my pain condition. My pain condition…is completely unique and complex, as it is with every human being. His genuine concern and attention to my words put me at ease.

I expressed to him my initial fears and concerns about the treatment working or providing some relief. After listening to me, he began to openly share with me that my pain relief would fully depend on me and my whole physical body. He explained to me that acupuncture differs from traditional medicine in the fact that it addresses the body holistically. It focuses on the entire "whole" being of a person—the mind, body, and soul.

As he began to elaborate on this alternative therapy, he was very direct in telling me that my results would be in direct correlation to my faith and belief in accepting relief.

He said, "Patients who have faith and believe in this therapy typically experience tremendous results and relief." Let me just tell you, I was ready for relief!

I can now say that I am no longer afraid of needles! The application of this ancient Chinese medicine and the wisdom that it contains drastically changed the way that I dealt with my pain. After my first session, I immediately began experiencing shifts of the energy flow in my body. My mind, body, and soul were now on a mission to get into the "flow" and rebalance their own unique energies. I felt completely "alive" and "awakened." My world began to expand.

Holistic Living

Empowered with a renewed sense of energy and hope, I began researching holistic living. I was now ready to enter into a completely different realm—mentally, physically, and spiritually. I knew deep in my soul that I had just been "awakened" to discover the truth. This was the beginning of my enlightenment. This new journey that I was so passionately set out on...was just the beginning.

This new life that I was about to live was completely different from my past life. It required me to live in a manner that honored my whole self as a person, which meant recognizing and honoring my mind, body, and soul as well as their direct relation and effects upon one another. This new holistic lifestyle was based on balancing all of these vital aspects in my life in order for me to live as my best self. Are you ready to live holistically and live your best life now?

Holistic living will allow you to discover the joy of living a wholesome life by restoring a balance between your mind, body, and soul. This restoration will result in an abundance of love, happiness, health, prosperity and spiritual fulfillment. Living a holistic lifestyle requires that you to live in balance with yourself, others, and the world around you. You must fully come to the realization that all things are interconnected. This requires you to take full responsibility for your own actions and choices in "knowing" that your personal decisions have a direct impact on yourself, humanity, and the world at large. You must deeply respect that the value of the whole of an entity is greater than the sum of its parts.

Through living this new lifestyle, you will be able to discover, claim, and live your true potential, passion, and power. This will enable you to bless and encourage others while bringing your own unique gifts and talents into the world. It will cause your heart to change. You will begin placing a much higher importance on your own personal values as well as the qualities and characteristics of yourself and others. Your sole mission and purpose on this earth will be to "Live to Love." This life will be your new reality with "Love Vision."

You will be greatly inspired to reach out to those who aren't "Love Visionaries" and share with them the power, grace, and hope that is available to them. Those living a life of "Love Vision" will outshine the ways of those living in our "SSS."

Forgiveness and Faith Are Requirements of Love Vision

In order to get your "Love Vision" on, you must learn how to forgive. Without forgiveness, there is no hope. We must choose to show love and compassion to ourselves, others, and our world. Forgiveness is one of the biggest gifts that we can give ourselves. It grants us the opportunity to daily stop judging and condemning. It grants us a renewed sense of hope.

If we are unwilling to forgive, we will be held hostage to strong feelings of guilt, sadness, anger, and resentment. These emotions will hold us captive and imprison us from living our lives to the fullest. Not choosing forgiveness will ultimately rob us of our future. Many people live their lives full of guilt, shame, anger, resentment, and discontent due to the nature of their hearts. They're unable to ever move forward in their lives because of a lack of forgiveness for themselves and others. If we choose forgiveness, we will be able to live lives full of freedom, abundance, and blessings.

Forgiveness requires faith in order to move forward. Faith is a companion of forgiveness. Faith is the ability to believe. We must believe that we can do all things. We must believe in a power greater than ourselves. This power will give us direction, purpose, and passion. It will grant us a renewed sense of peace, hope, strength, gratitude, courage, and joy. This power will enable us to reconnect with ourselves, our inherent truth, and others.

Things Aren't Always As They Appear to Be

What I've learned from my personal experience and pain is that things aren't always as they appear to be. Everyone in this world is silently suffering. You, your friends, your acquaintances, and all the other people in this world are suffering. This is a fact. As humans, when we enter into this world, we are entering into a world of pain and suffering. Life is a giver of pleasure and pain and is a journey for every individual who is given the opportunity to live.

The problem that we face is that we tend to view people with only our physical vision; as a result, this forces our egos to judge people and determine their value and worth. For example, many of us look at other people and think that they have the "perfect lives." We assume this based upon their appearance, wealth, fame, status, lifestyle, career, relationships, etc…But these assumptions that our egos create are false lies.

We tend to develop hate in our hearts toward others when we are mistreated by them. We label them as rude, mean, angry, hateful, b*tchy, *sshole, etc….But the truth is that we don't know what these people are going through in their personal lives. We don't know the pain that they're experiencing. Most of the time, when people treat others poorly, they are projecting their pain. They are in such deep suffering that they live in a way that projects their pain onto others. As a result, the person who they mistreat is hurt, and more pain is inflicted. This is a vicious cycle. This cycle kills, steals, and destroys the lives of many.

It's time for us to open the eyes of our hearts and start viewing ourselves, others, and the world from a place of love! When we do this, our vision will be altered, and we will start to view things on a completely different level. We will begin to see from the eyes of our hearts. This new perspective will allow us to gain deep insight and awareness regarding the pain in our lives, in others' lives, and in the world. Once we are able to see things clearly, our hearts will begin to change. We will then have the desire to nurture, love, respect, and care for ourselves and one another. As a result, we will be able to unite together to help each other heal the pain that we all are suffering from—physically, emotionally, mentally, psychologically, and spiritually.

CHAPTER 6

The Power of Acceptance

WE NEED TO work on developing the habit of looking at whatever happens to us through a positive mind-set. Life brings us many challenges that are very difficult to embrace when we are suffering. But if we begin practicing acceptance, we will be able to cope with our challenges and crises in a different way. This will allow us to gain new perspectives that will enable us to take action in our lives to change our current reality. When we accept challenges, we are able to see the positive and choose a peaceful state of mind. When we choose the opposite and resist, we end up being miserable as we struggle against the Universe.

Living in our "SSS," we are brainwashed to not accept ourselves. The media utilizes the power of its various outlets through television, movies, radio, billboards, magazines, the Internet, and social media to communicate with you on a daily basis. The media is very sneaky…Its message is both subliminal and direct in telling you that you're not good enough, attractive enough, smart enough, happy enough, rich enough, successful enough, etc…The "SSS" makes you feel as though you're living in a state of lack and that you need to change yourself. It plays on your insecurities, doubts, and fears in order to make you feel inadequate, unhappy, and powerless. Its goal is to make you live in a state of denial and rejection of yourself, so you will feel insecure in your own identity. When it has this control over you, you become powerless and victimized to brainwashing. The "SSS" is then able to accomplish its mission of successfully communicating with you. It tells you exactly how you need to act and live your life and what you need to do and buy in order to be happy and complete.

The "SSS" offers you a variety of solutions and outlets to help you numb your pain, physically, mentally, emotionally, and spiritually. These solutions and outlets will only temporarily numb your pain and suffering. Many of them are traps that can lead you to a life full of addiction. When you become a victim of the "SSS," it's very easy for you to lose sight of your true identity, goals, vision, and ability to speak your "authentic truth." When you're victimized, you are wearing the "SSS" blinders and are unable to see the truth and live a life full of passion and purpose. You become easily distracted and remain at an extremely high risk to begin taking steps that will ultimately deter you from following your God-given path to fulfill your destiny.

But...I am here to tell you that it is time for you to "WAKE UP" and to rip off the "SSS" blinders that you're wearing! It's not too late for you to make the decision to put on your "Love Vision" glasses and begin living in a state of truth, love, and self-acceptance. When you "WAKE UP" and remove your "SSS" blinders, you will begin to see clearly. Choosing to wear your "Love Vision" glasses daily will allow you to change the course of your destiny. This new perspective will grant you the incredible power of self-acceptance. It will allow you to surrender and accept yourself, the people, places, and circumstances in your life. Acceptance will allow you to live fully present in your life. It will give you the permission to love yourself, others, and the world around you. This doesn't mean that you will become complacent. It actually means the complete opposite. For when we refuse to accept ourselves, others, and life's circumstances...we are fighting against our own reality. When we do this, we become very unhappy because of feelings of shame, anger, fear, guilt, and hate that are controlling our state of being. But if we choose to accept our current reality, we will be given a power that will allow us to change the courses of our lives. This power is the power of love. When we choose to love ourselves, others, and our present lives, we are choosing love over hate. Love is the most powerful force in the Universe. Nothing is impossible with love. For when we start living a life of love, miracles begin happening.

Your new perception of love will allow you to take action in your life that will enable you to create positive change. Expansion will begin to happen as you free yourself from your limiting emotions, thoughts, and beliefs. Opportunities will begin presenting themselves regularly as you begin living in a state of love that supports yourself, others, and the world around you. So instead of staring at any closed doors in front of you or getting tired and bruised while trying to break them down, you will turn around and see the many other open doors that are surrounding you....just waiting for you to enter. As you begin consciously walking in a state of love, you will be guided step-by-step to take the path that will ultimately lead you to fulfill your destiny.

The Serenity Prayer

God grant me the serenity to accept the things I cannot change; Courage to change the things I can; And wisdom to know the difference.

—REINHOLD NEIBUHR (1892-1971)

The Power of Adaptation

Through engaging in the process of acceptance and self-love, you will be granted the strength, courage, and wisdom to recognize the changes that you need to make in yourself and in your life in order to create change and begin living a life that you love. Change is not easy. Period...End of story. But you need to ask yourself the following questions: If I don't make changes in my life, what will happen? If everything stays the same, will I be happy and fulfilled?

You know the answers to these questions. Deep down, you know that change is necessary in order for you to move forward in your life and begin creating and living the life that you are meant to live.

If you don't create change in your life, change will create you. The fact is…that change itself is constant, whether we want to admit it or not. This is part of life. Even if you try to resist or avoid it, change will enter your life. Since change is inevitable, it is much better for you to be proactive and begin creating changes yourself. It will be much easier for you to adapt because the changes you initiate will be ones that you desire. Once we start identifying what we need to change in ourselves and in our lives, we will need to adapt. When we accept the things that we can't change and those things that we have no control over, we are able to adapt to our current circumstances and begin creating a new way to live our lives.

There is great power in adaptation. Adaptation is the power that makes things happen, regardless of your circumstances. Since you are a "Student of Love," I'm going to reference the *Merriam-Webster* definition of adaptation: (1) the act or process of changing to better suit a situation, (2) a body part or feature or a behavior that helps a living thing survive and function better in its environment, and (3) the process of changing to fit some purpose or situation or the process of adapting. I especially like the third definition, which stresses that the process of changing is to fit a purpose. Being a "Student of Love" and "Love Visionary," you have a very specific purpose! Your purpose is to create and live a life you love, one that will change the lives of many. Your purpose is God-given and you were created to live this purpose with passion and fulfill a legacy that only you can create.

Adaptation is a requirement for all "Love Visionaries." Life is full of challenges and setbacks, many of which are the difficult circumstances, situations, and people that come into your life. Others are the financial, mental, emotional, psychological, or physical health problems that you may be facing. Regardless, you have the strength to accept the things that you can't change, and you have the power to begin changing what you can to create a better life. The *Merriam-Webster* gives some great synonyms that describe what adaptation truly is and how you can apply it in your life. Here are some of my favorite synonyms for adaptation: alteration, modification, redesign, remodeling, revamping, reworking, reconstruction, conversion, adjustment, acclimation, accommodations, acculturation, assimilation, and integration. All of these actions in their various forms will help you move from living in a state of "surviving" to living in a state of "thriving." These actions are not for the weak of heart! You must remain strong and committed to your purpose and vision. You will be required to get comfortable living in the uncomfortable and outside of your comfort zone.

It is in this process of adaptation that you will learn how to live flexibly, creatively, and fully in the present moment. Living in this manner will allow you to live in a state of "flow" so that you can maintain peace and balance in your life, regardless of your circumstances. When you consciously make the decision and commitment to accept yourself and your current reality, you're opening up the space needed for you to adapt your behavior, environment, current circumstances, and actions in order to create massive change. A vital component of adaptation is that it requires you to change your mind-set, thoughts, emotions, beliefs, habits, behaviors and actions to align with your goals and dreams. You must work hard every single day at aligning these powerful forces with the outcomes that you desire so that you can create your vision. You must strategically choose your thoughts, emotions, beliefs, habits, behaviors, and actions, for they will determine how you live your daily life. Ultimately, they will shape your destiny. In doing so, you will become the best version of yourself. You will be able to live freely and fully, creating a life that you love.

Creation requires unprecedented action, commitment, behavior modification, dedication, and perseverance. You need to be open and honest. Ask yourself how serious you are about making lasting and positive changes in your life. Once you're able to answer this and commit to adapting your thoughts, beliefs, mind-set, habits, behaviors, and actions to align with your vision, you will begin living your best life now. Through the process of removing the self-imposed limiting beliefs, thoughts, and emotions that have been holding you back, you will gain a new perspective that will enable you to see numerous new opportunities that surround you. You will begin to realize that these opportunities are the various avenues that will allow you to accomplish your goals. Your "Love Vision" will allow you to fully comprehend that there are many different ways in which you can live your life.

The decision is up to you and you only. If you feel as though you're on a hamster wheel in your life, going nowhere...or if every day feels like groundhog day....It is time to make MASSIVE CHANGES in your life! For the wise Albert Einstein once said, "The definition of insanity is doing something over and over again and expecting a different result." For if you truly desire MASSIVE CHANGE in your life, then it's time to get serious and start living a life full of MASSIVE CHANGE on a daily basis. Don't let your current circumstances and your past define you, your present reality, and your future. It's time for you to reclaim your own power and to start making change an integral part of your daily life, so you can start living your best life now. You only have one life to live. Don't waste any time. Start now, and make it your best life ever!

Words of Wisdom on Change

The secret of change is to focus all of your energy not on fighting the old, but on building the new.

—SOCRATES

Change the changeable, accept the unchangeable, and remove yourself from the unacceptable.

—DENIS WAITLEY

Change your thoughts and your change your world.

—NORMAN VINCENT PEALE

For every positive change you make in your life, something else also changes for the better—it creates a chain reaction.

—LEON BROWN

If you change the way you look at things, the things you look at change.

—DR. WAYNE DYER

Any change, even a change for the better, is always accompanied by drawbacks and discomforts.

—ARNOLD BENNETT

Progress is impossible without change, and those who cannot change their minds cannot change anything.

—GEORGE BERNARD SHAW

Life is 10% what happens to me and 90% of how I react to it.

—JOHN C. MAXWELL

Work joyfully and peacefully, knowing that right thoughts and right efforts inevitably bring about right results.

—JAMES ALLEN

Every positive change in your life begins with a clear, unequivocal decision that you are going to either do something or stop doing something.

—BRIAN TRACY

Optimist are usually wrong. But all the great change in history, positive change, was done by optimists.

—THOMAS FRIEDMAN

Learning is the first step in making positive changes within yourself. Other factors are conviction, determination, action, and effort. Learning and education help develop conviction about the need to change and increase your commitment. Conviction then develops into determination. Next, strong determination leads to action: a sustained effort to implement the changes. This final factor of effort is critical.

—DALAI LAMA

Once you replace negative thoughts with positive ones, you'll start having positive results.

—WILLIE NELSON

My all-time favorite topic in positive psychology is the study of positive emotions. I'm fascinated by how pleasant experiences, which can be so subtle and fleeting, can add up over time to change who we become. I'm especially excited these days about investigating how positive emotions change the very ways that our cells form and function to keep us healthy.

—BARBARA FREDRICKSON

Be the change that you wish to see in the world.

—MAHATMA GANDHI

The world as we have created it is a process of our thinking. It cannot be changed without changing our thinking.

—ALBERT EINSTEIN

Change is inevitable. Change is constant.

—BENJAMIN DISRAELI

If we don't change, we don't grow. If we don't grow, we aren't really living.

—GAIL SHEEHY

Change is the law of life. And those who look only to the past or present are certain to miss the future.

—JOHN F. KENNEDY

Transform the world by transforming yourself.

—DAVIDJI

When I let go of Who I am, I become Who I might be.

—LAO TZU

CHAPTER 7

The Power of Purpose

As a "Love Visionary," your purpose is to live a life of love. In a world full of darkness and despair, you're required to be the light. It is your responsibility to give faith, hope, and love to others through your actions and by the way you live your life. Every "Love Visionary" has a different life purpose that he or she is called to fulfill based upon his or her unique gifts, blessings, and talents. You must discover what your purpose is, for this is your life's mission.

Purpose is the structure on which you build your life. It is a direct expression of your VISION, values, beliefs, and passions. It is the drive that makes you want to get up in the morning and add value into the world. You need to ask yourself the following questions: "Am I living a purpose-driven life?" and, "Do I live a life of meaning, purpose, joy, and passion?" If you answered no to either one of these questions, then it's time for you to discover your purpose. Purpose is all about finding your authentic self by discovering what you truly love and are passionate about and then committing to living in a way that honors that. It is about discovering the things that make you feel inspired, motivated, peaceful, and happy. These are the things that will allow you to live a longer, healthier, and happier life.

An Important Message to You about Your "Love Vision" Journal

My dear "Love Visionary,".....*Love Vision* is more than just a book! This is your space for discovery, exploration, and creation! You are about to delve into the realm of "Powerful

Questioning" and personal-discovery exercises to help you get your "Love Vision" on! Your built-in "Love Vision" journal and workbook will give you the space to freely express your innermost struggles, fears, and pain as well as your deepest desires, goals, and dreams. It has been designed to help you gain clarity regarding your life's purpose and passion.

Some of the questions throughout "Love Vision" that I will ask you may seem repetitive or similar in nature. Answer these questions, as they will truly grant you insight, wisdom, and guidance. You must open your heart and mind to freely express yourself, so you can begin to build a life that you love. It is your canvas for creation....Let it inspire, motivate, and encourage you. Your "Love Vision" journal will serve as your personal blueprint for building your dream life. Grab a pen—it's time to get started!

Exercise: Discovering Your Purpose

You need to dig deep within your soul and ask yourself the below questions. They will help you to gain clarity regarding your life's true purpose.

1. What do I feel I was born to do?

2. What am I passionate about and love doing?

3. What skills, gifts, and talents do I naturally possess that I could use to help others and make a difference in this world?

4. If I could be remembered for only three things after I die, what would they be?

You were born for so much more than to just go to work every day, be stressed, earn money, pay your bills, retire, and die. You were born to be the most authentic and whole version of you that you can possibly be. The more that you live in a manner that supports who you truly are—and the more that you're able to live out your authentic truth—the more you will be able to utilize your skills, talents, strengths, and gifts to help others and live a life that you truly love. When you're aligned with your purpose, your life will be full of joy, peace, excitement, fulfillment, and passion. Why? Because passion and purpose go hand in hand! Pursuing what you truly love will give you an unwavering sense of direction in your life that will fuel your inner fire and propel you forward to accomplishing your purpose.

It's up to you to discover your passions and live what you truly love to do! Passion and purpose are the foundation of success in every area of your life. They will allow you to prosper physically, emotionally, mentally, spiritually, and financially. They will enable you to build amazing relationships with your friends, family, colleagues, contacts, and even strangers. Passion and purpose are the key ingredients to living a life full of freedom and abundance. Every morning when you wake up, you need to ask yourself, "What is my purpose?" This is what will give your life true meaning, fulfillment, and passion, so you can create a vision and plan that will allow for you to fulfill your God-given destiny. Allow your purpose to serve as your compass, for it will help guide you step-by-step to living the life of your wildest dreams!

Words of Wisdom on Purpose

The purpose of life is to live it, to taste experience to the utmost,
to reach out eagerly and without fear for newer and
richer experience.

—ELEANOR ROOSEVELT

The mystery of human existence lies not in just staying alive, but in finding
something to live for.

—FYODOR DOSTOYEVSKY

You were put on this earth to achieve your greatest self, to live out your purpose, and to do it courageously.

—Steve Maraboli

The purpose of life is a life of purpose.

—Robert Bryne

A good book is the precious life-blood of a master-spirit, embalmed and treasured up on purpose to a life beyond life, and as such it must surely be a necessary commodity.

—Penelope Fitzgerald

But beware of this about callings: they may not lead us where we intended to go or even where we want to go. If we choose to follow, we may have to be willing to let go of the life we already planned and accept whatever is waiting for us. And if the calling is true, though we may not have gone where we intended, we will surely end up where we need to be.

—Steve Goodier

Everything in this world happens with a purpose. You are born in this world with a purpose, you are chosen by purpose.

—Udai Yadla

You were put on this earth to achieve your greatest self, to live out your purpose, and to do it courageously.

—Dr. Steve Maraboli

Life without purpose is like a body without a soul.

—TASNEEM HAMEED

If you can't figure out your purpose, figure out your passion. For your passion will lead you right into your purpose.

—BISHOP T.D. JAKES

The best day of your life is the one on which you decide your life is your own. No apologies or excuses. No one to lean on, rely on, or blame. The gift is yours—it is an amazing journey—and you alone are responsible for the quality of it. This is the day your life really begins.

—BOB MOAWAD

Your purpose in life is to find the LOVE within you, surrender yourself to it and then share it with others.

—ALLSON

Our purpose on earth is not to reach some light at the end of the tunnel. Our greatest to-do in this life time is to practice our most burning passion to the best of our ability. We deserve to be alive—every second of the day, and at the end of our journey, look back and say, "I F*CKING lived and it was beautiful."

—ANDREA BALT

The Power of Commitment

What is commitment? Learnersdictionary.com defines commitment as the following: "a promise to do or give, a promise to be loyal to someone or something, and the attitude of someone who works very hard to do or support something." Are you living a life that is committed to your purpose, passions, and vision? Living a life of commitment is the act of sincerely putting your heart into everything that you do, with the purpose of manifesting your goals and vision. Commitment is doing whatever is needed for as long as necessary in order to get SH*T done! When you are truly committed, you will be granted a magical power that will allow you to achieve your goals.

Commitment is more than doing that which is easy, convenient, and comfortable. It comes with a price. You must be willing to make many sacrifices in order to achieve success. This is not a temporary process. It is a continuous, moment-by-moment undertaking that requires your mind, body, and soul to be 100 percent dedicated to your purpose. You must relentlessly pursue actions that are aligned to your purpose in order to manifest your dreams. Success is achieved when you choose to live in this manner.

The real difference between excellence and mediocrity is commitment. It is those who give their goals focused action and commitment who eventually end up manifesting their dreams. No matter how big or small their goals and dreams are…they focus their attention, action, and commitment on creating the VISION that they have for their lives. They are successful because they're dedicated to the entire process of success. This includes setting goals, strategizing an action plan, working their A** off, and persistently working through all of the challenges until dreams become reality. Commitment is a decision that you can make for yourself at any given time, regardless of your past, present, and current circumstances. When you choose to live a life of commitment and purpose, power is then placed in your hands. It is time for you to reclaim your own power and to daily commit to living out all of the exciting possibilities and opportunities that are available to you, today and every day. You were born to live a life you love, one of freedom, fulfillment, and abundance. Commit to living your best life now. You're deserve it!

Words of Wisdom on Commitment

Commitment is what turns a promise into reality.

—ABRAHAM LINCOLN

The quality of a person's life is in direct proportion to their commitment to excellence, regardless of their chosen field of endeavor.

—VINCE LOMBARDI

Individuals who succeed have a belief in the power of commitment.
If there's a single belief that seems almost inseparable from success,
it's that there's no great success without commitment. If you look at successful
people in any field, you'll find they're not necessarily the best and the brightest,
the fastest and the strongest. You'll find they're the ones
with the most commitment.

—TONY ROBBINS

There's a difference between interest and commitment. When you're interested in doing something, you do it only when it's convenient. When you're committed to something, you accept no excuses; only results.

—Kenneth Blanchard

I will not be distracted by noise, chatter, or setbacks. Patience, commitment, grace, and purpose will guide me.

—Louise Hay

Desire is the key to motivation, but it's determination and commitment to an unrelenting pursuit of your goal a commitment to excellence that will enable you to attain the success you seek.

—Mario Andretti

Unless commitment is made, there are only promises and hopes; but no plans.

—Peter F. Drucker

Set the standard! Stop expecting others to show you love, acceptance, commitment, and respect when you don't even show that to yourself.

—Steve Maraboli

Make a Commitment to be absolutely faithful to that which exists nowhere but within yourself.

—Dr. Wayne Dyer

Freedom is not the absence of commitments, but the ability to choose and commit myself to what is best for me.

—Paulo Coelho

Commitment is an act, not a word.

—Jean-Paul Sartre

Commitment unlocks the doors of imagination, allows vision, and gives us the right stuff to turn our dream into reality.

—James Womack

Commitment is the ultimate assertion of human freedom. It releases all the energy you possess and enables you to take quantum leaps in creativity. When you set a one-pointed intention and absolutely refuse to allow obstacles to dissipate the focused quality of your attention, you engage the infinite organizing power of the Universe.

—Deepak Chopra

The Power of Living in the Present

We live in a day and age that is nonstop. The past decade has produced unprecedented advances with regard to the Internet, social media, cell phones, and other technology that all offer us various ways to connect with others—no matter where we are in the world. We now have the ability to constantly connect, communicate, and create in ways that we had only dreamed of before. We are truly blessed to be living in such an exciting era that offers us unlimited opportunities to create, cultivate, and connect.

We are constantly emailing, texting, Facebooking, Instagramming, Snapchatting, tweeting, etc…But are these various communication channels truly allowing us to connect with ourselves, others, and the world around us? Many of us have allowed these communication outlets to take control over our lives. We have become so consumed with the messages from our pop culture, "SSS," the Internet, social media, etc…that we have lost our true connection with ourselves and the ability to live fully present in our own lives. We are all so concerned with connecting via social media outlets that we, ironically, have disconnected. We have such a hard time sitting still and being present in the moment because we are always focusing on something else. This disconnect has affected all of our generation. We are living in a state of "constant contact," unable to live in the present moment. Our minds are constantly racing as to what we need to do next. Through our constant efforts to connect and communicate, we somehow lost our sense of awareness.

Think about this….How often are you fully engaged in the present moment? Most people ignore it, preoccupied with the thinking of their busy minds, dwelling both on the past and future. Humans rely on "thinking" as a means to work out their lives. This forces them into focusing their thoughts, emotions, energy, and attention on their doubts, insecurities, struggles, challenges…etc…ALL OF THE NEGATIVE. This negative thinking becomes a mental, emotional, spiritual, and physical downward spiral that forces people to live in states of anxiety and fear. As a result, most of our society today is living on autopilot. We're running on a hamster wheel of endless "busy-ness," not knowing how to stop. Our days are completely consumed with our jobs, routines, and responsibilities. Time seems as though it is flying by as our days turn into weeks, which turn into months, which then turn into years. Many of our biggest desires and dreams seem to slip away as the sand passes through the hourglass of our lives. We are so busy that we feel as though we can't live in the present moment; we are always thinking about and planning the next thing that we need to do or accomplish. When we live in this manner, we end up adopting a very hectic lifestyle that ultimately leads us to living lives of anxiety, confusion, depression, and emptiness. This is not the life that you were meant to live.

You were born to live a life of FREEDOM—one fully in the present, so you can live your best life now! When you begin living in the present moment, you truly start LIVING. You will begin to experience fulfillment, peace, joy, abundance, and love in ways that you never have before. Living in the present moment will bring calm, peace, and serenity into your life…even amid the storms and challenges that may come your way. This is the beginning of conscious living; it allows you to live at one with the present rather than being controlled by your ego. The more you start living in the present moment, the more "awareness" you will begin to have in your life. You must learn how to live mindfully and how to incorporate mindfulness into your daily life.

What is mindfulness? Mindfulness is when you consciously choose to focus your attention on the present moment in a manner that is nonjudgmental. This gives you the opportunity to become aware of your mental, emotional, spiritual, and physical states without judgment. It allows you to gain clarity on the pain or frustration that you're feeling. Through being aware of your inner states of well-being, you will be able to reconnect with yourself and begin healing the suffering in your life. Mindfulness gives you the power to heal yourself by allowing you to give yourself compassion, understanding, and love. Your heart will begin to open as you reconnect with your authentic self, others, and the world around you. Living in this state of "awareness" will allow you to feel completely "ALIVE"! For when you live in the beauty of the present, you're able to live in pure freedom. You're given the unstoppable power to create your own reality.

Words of Wisdom on Living in the Present

Do not dwell in the past, do not dream of the future, concentrate the mind on the present moment.

—BUDDHA

The point of power is always in the present moment.

—Louise L. Hay

Life gives you plenty of time to do whatever you want to do if you stay in the present moment.

—Deepak Chopra

The present moment, if you think about it, is the only time there is. No matter what time it is, it is always now.

—Marianne Williamson

A great hallmark of mental wellness is the ability to be in the present moment, fully and with no thoughts of being elsewhere.

—Wayne Dyer

If you are depressed, you are living in the past. If you're anxious, you are living in the future. If you are at peace, you are living in the present moment.

—Lao Tzu

Words of Wisdom from Eckhart Tolle

Realize deeply that the present moment is all you ever have. Make the Now the primary focus of your life.

When you take your attention into the present moment, a certain alertness arises. You become more conscious of what's around you, but also, strangely, a sense of presence that is both within and without.

It is through gratitude for the present moment that the spiritual dimension of life opens up.

The answer is, who you are cannot be defined through thinking or mental labels or definitions, because it's beyond that. It is the very sense of being, or presence, that is there when you become conscious of the present moment. In essence, you and what we call the present moment are, at the deepest level, one.

Don't wait to be successful at some future point. Have a successful relationship with the present moment and be fully present in whatever you are doing. That is success.

Your entire life only happens in this moment. The present moment is life itself. Yet, people live as if the opposite were true and treat the present moment as a stepping stone to the next moment—a means to an end.

Most people treat the present moment as if it were an obstacle that they need to overcome. Since the present moment is life itself, it is an insane way to live.

Always say "yes" to the present moment...Surrender to what is. Say "yes" to life—and see how life starts suddenly to start working for you rather than against you.

Mindful Exercise: "Be Where You Are"

The "Be Where You Are" mindful exercises are designed to help you begin practicing mindfulness in your daily life. They will allow you to have intentional, nonjudgmental awareness so that you can live moment by moment and experience life to the fullest. It is scientifically proven that mindfulness and meditation have countless health benefits, including reducing depression, anxiety, and stress; controlling disease and pain management; helping with one's sleep patterns; aiding substance-abuse problems and eating disorders, etc…Mindfulness improves our overall health and well-being—physically, mentally, emotionally, psychologically, and spiritually. As a result, this helps us to build up stronger immune systems so that we can live healthier, happier, and more fulfilled lives.

Are you ready to engage in mindful living? The below exercises are awesome because they work! They will help you to de-stress, unplug, and re-energize so that you can live more fully present in your own life. Don't worry…they are super easy to fit into your normal daily routine; you can do them literally anywhere at any given time to help you get your "ZEN ON"!

1. **Be aware of your senses**. Be fully aware of all that you can see, hear, smell, taste, and feel. Pay attention to all of your senses, and you'll start experiencing life like you never have before!

2. **Be aware of your breath**. All you need to do is remain present and focus on your breath for just one minute. Start by breathing in and out slowly, with each breath cycle lasting around six or seven seconds. Breathe in through your nose, and exhale your breath through your mouth. Allow your breath to flow freely in and out of your body. Completely let go of your thoughts, and focus on your breath as it enters through your nose and exits your mouth. Notice how the air moves through your chest and abdomen. Purposefully watch your breath, and let it go. Let go of all of the thoughts, anxiety, and stress that is weighing you down. Let each new breath bring life to your mind, body, and soul. Allow your breath to calm, restore, and reenergize you to live your healthiest self now!

3. **Be aware of nature.** You must learn how to be completely present in your life so that you can enjoy the beauty of all the nature that surrounds you! Incorporate

time spent in nature in your day. Even if you only have five or ten minutes to spare, take this time to spend in nature. Be creative….Here are some ideas: start drinking your morning coffee outside on your patio, take your lunch break outside, practice mindfulness on your way home from work, take a walk in the evening to enjoy the beauty that surrounds you, make it a point to watch early sunrises and evening sunsets, and bask in stargazing. These are only a few of the many different ways that you can incorporate spending time in nature on a daily basis. When you're outside, pay attention to the birds chirping, notice the different colored leaves and trees, and hear the whistling of the wind. Do you hear traffic, people engaging in conversation, dogs barking, or children playing? Allow yourself to feel the air gracefully touching your skin and the sun's rays warming your entire body. No matter what natural activity you choose to engage in, just make sure that you remain fully present in the moment so that you can be aware of all of the natural beauty that surrounds you.

4. **Be aware of what you hear.** Sometimes…or should I say most of the time… our minds are so busy and preoccupied that we aren't truly engaging in "ACTIVE LISTENING" in our lives. You need to learn how to practice "ACTIVE LISTENING" because this will allow you to be fully present in your daily interactions with others and the world around you. When someone is speaking, whether to you directly or to others, focus your attention on actively listening by fully concentrating on what is being said rather than just passively hearing the words of the person. Active listening requires that you listen with all of your senses. You need to give your full attention and awareness to focusing on what the person is trying to communicate. You need to express your awareness and interest by using both verbal and nonverbal messages such as nodding your head, smiling, or just commenting and acknowledging what they say. When you remain fully present in your interactions with others and actively listen to them, you are opening up space for better communication. This will allow you to connect better with yourself, others, and the world around you; you will be more authentically engaged.

5. **Be aware of what you can be grateful for.** Every day, make it a habit to notice five different things in your day that you are grateful for. These may even be the things that you usually take for granted or may not even notice are a blessing. Pay attention throughout the course of your day, and pick five things. They can be people, places, or things. It's totally up to you to identify five different things each day that you are grateful for. Practicing this exercise on a daily basis will help you to start paying attention to all of the things that make your life special. It's about noticing both the big and even the small (unique) things that add life and love to your day.

6. **Be immersed in your daily life.** One of the most powerful mindfulness practices we can adopt is to start immersing ourselves fully into our own lives by fully engaging our minds, bodies, and souls into all that it is we do. Since our minds have become programmed to constantly race and think about all of the things that we need to do, this practice is vital to incorporate into our daily lives if we want to live fully in the present. The goal of "MINDFUL IMMERSION" is to cultivate contentment in the present moment, regardless of what you're doing. Whether it be your daily responsibilities, activities, chores, work, or your interactions with your friends, family, coworkers, and strangers…completely immerse yourself—your mind, body, and soul—to be present in that situation. Take your regular work responsibilities and communication interactions, for example….Instead of anxiously wanting to complete these obligations and quickly finish the tasks at hand, allow yourself to be fully present and live in the moment…..Being AWARE, ALERT, and ACTIVELY engaging in your life…will allow you to begin experiencing life like you never have before. Your mind, body, and soul will be fully engaged in living in the present moment so that you can live your life to the fullest!

CHAPTER 8

The Power of Creating Your Own RULES

WHAT EXACTLY ARE RULES? How do you define rules? Well....when in doubt, I always turn to good old *Merriam-Webster* to give me clear and concise definitions. Here are my three top favorite definitions of the word "rule" from Merriam-Webster.com: (1) a pre-scribed guide for conduct or action; (2) an accepted procedure, custom, or habit; and (3) the exercise of authority or control, dominion.

From the time that you were born, you have been taught rules. "Don't cry!" "You must say please and thank you," "Look both ways before crossing the street," "Always wear your helmet when riding your bike," "Clean your room," and "Raise your hand if you want to ask a question." As you got older, the rules changed.....although they continued. "You must wear your seatbelt whenever you're in a car," "Stop at stop signs and red lights," "Make sure you always use condoms when you have sex," and "Don't drink and drive." You were taught rules in every area of your life: school rules, sports rules, food rules, family rules, friend rules, cleaning rules, and even stranger rules. All of these rules served a distinct purpose in order to help guide and protect you as you lived your life. They provided a framework for you regarding what was and what wasn't acceptable. They were expectations that you were required to meet. These rules provided a sense of order and structure in your life in order to prevent any chaos, confusion, or catas-trophes. Overall, these rules kept you safe! Thank God for rules, for without them.... disorder, danger, and discord result. Rules definitely serve an extremely important and vital purpose in our lives.

The majority of the basic rules that you were taught when you were younger were good. They were simple directions to help guide and protect you. Although as you got older… much older…you began to let the opinions, beliefs, thoughts, and words of others rule your life. As a result, you gave up your free will to develop your own personalized rules for your life. This is so sad! All of your life, you were taught rules to follow….and now that you're finally grown and have the freedom to create your own rules and to live life the way you truly desire…you have decided to give up your power! Hello!?!?!? It's time for you to WAKE UP!!!! You have become a prisoner and victim to the opinions, beliefs, thoughts, and words of others. Seriously….think about it! You know that it is true… at least to some degree. If I were to ask you right now what your personal rules are for your life, would you be able to tell me what they are? Really think about this: Have you established your own personal rules in which to live your life by? If you answered no or even maybe to this question, then it's time for you to reclaim your power and to develop the most important rules that you will ever follow in your life.

The new rules that you need to create are your "LOVE VISION" RULES that will enable you to live a life that you love! These rules will provide you with more fun, flexibility, and freedom in your life. You're a "Love Visionary," and developing your "LOVE VISION" RULES is a nonnegotiable! If you want to build a life that you absolutely love, you must dedicate the time to developing the rules that will allow you to fulfill your VISION. If you decide not to create and implement your own rules, you will be living a life according to the rules of someone else. You're the CEO of your life! It's time for you to "OWN" it, and start acting like it! If you're unhappy in any area of your life, change it. You're the BOSS! You are responsible for calling the shots! Be your most authentic self. Speak your truth. Your authenticity is the best designer brand that you own. Wear it every day, and wear it well.

You need to begin by setting your personal standards, requirements, and nonnegotiables for every single area of your life. I'm talking about what you expect from your work at school, your job, career, relationships (friends, family, romantic relationships, work relationships), health and wellness, finances, success, your spiritual life, etc....you need to develop rules for all of the various areas of your life. Next, you need to implement these rules by aligning your daily thoughts, words, actions, behaviors, habits, and values to match them. In doing this, you will be able to live your best life now and manifest your goals, desires, and dreams.

When you develop and implement your own "LOVE VISION" RULES to live by, you will put yourself in a league that is so substantially different and unique from all the other players! People will be dying to know what your core fundamentals, values, and principles are. You will emerge as a thought leader, activist, and leading "Love Visionary." People will want to know what it is that you possess so that they also can live a life full of abundance, freedom, peace, passion, and happiness.

By now...you know that I truly love words of wisdom! Throughout *Love Vision*, you will find many wise words from others that I've chosen to share with you due to their utmost significance for your life. I am extremely passionate about sharing with you powerful "Words of Wisdom" that I know will provide you with the insight, clarity, and courage that you need in order to help you make the decisions that are right for you and your life. These words are grounded in truth, positivity, and strength to encourage you to be true to yourself, your goals, desires, and VISION. The goal of all of these "Words of Wisdom" is to uplift, motivate, and inspire you to take unprecedented action so that you can manifest your dreams, fulfill your VISION, and live fully a life you love.

Keep your thoughts positive because your thoughts become your words. Keep your words positive because your words become your behavior. Keep your behavior positive because your behavior becomes your habits. Keep your habits positive because your habits become your values. Keep your values positive because your values become your destiny.

—Mahatma Gandhi

The above "Words of Wisdom" are from Mahatma Gandhi and give you divine guidance regarding how you should live your life. I highly recommend that you read this several times and meditate on these words of truth. Use these "Words of Wisdom" as your foundation for building your own rules. Developing your own personal rules to live by is all about helping you to create a new lifestyle that is healthy for your mind, body, and soul. When you stand firm in your identity as a "Love Visionary," your life will be full of peace, balance, fulfillment, and joy. Now that you know the vital importance that rules play in your life, it's time for you to really "WAKE UP" and create the "LOVE VISION" RULES that will allow you to fulfill your destiny!

Exercise: Creating Your Personal "Love Vision" Rules

I have created a special acronym for the word rules in order to help you get started in developing your personal "LOVE VISION" RULES. I have chosen a specific description for each letter in the word RULES so that you can easily remember how important it is for you to implement your "LOVE VISION" RULES every day. Here it is: R (routines), U (you), L (live), E (everyday), and S (successfully and stress-free). I've listed a variety of the different areas that are in your life below.

Please make sure to add to the below list any other areas that you would like to develop rules for. All of the areas that I've listed below make up your life. Some of these you give your utmost attention, affection, and efforts—others, not so much. Some you ignore, and some you even avoid at all costs. With each area of your life that is listed below and with the ones that you choose to add to this list, you need to do three simple things for each area. First, you need to write down what you won't tolerate in this area of your life from yourself and others. Second, write what you expect from yourself and others in this specific area. Third, you need to write down what you aspire to achieve in this important area of your life. In doing this, you will be creating your own personal "LOVE VISION" RULES that will help you to develop the positive emotions, thoughts, words, actions, behaviors, habits, and values that will allow you to live your best life now. There is no need for you to settle! Ever! It's time for you to get clear, concise, and courageous! Grab your pen, and get ready to dig deep down into your soul….It's time for you to write out what you won't tolerate, what you expect, and what you desire to achieve in your life. Be real, open, and honest—you only have one life to live. This isn't a dress rehearsal.

Your Personal "LOVE VISION" RULES

1. School, job, career

2. Relationships

3. Physical health and wellness

4. Diet

5. Mental health

6. Emotional health

7. Spiritual life

8. Success

9. Finances

10. Leisure Time (Does this exist in your life? If you answered "NO" to this question…you better work hard at changing it! You deserve to relax, unwind, and spend time doing things that you love.)

11. Sleep

12. Creative time (time dedicated to creating your VISION)

Words of Wisdom on Living Life on Your Own Terms

Define success on your own terms, achieve it by your own rules, and build a life you're proud to live.

—ANNE SWEENEY

Do it on your own terms, not on anyone else's. This is your life and at the end of the day, you are responsible for your own happiness and your own decisions.

—ESENDEMIR SISTERS

If I had observed all the rules, I'd never have gotten anywhere.

—MARILYN MONROE

There are times when it will go so wrong that you will barely be alive, and times when you realize that being barely alive, on your own terms, is better than living a bloated half-life on someone else's terms.

—JEANETTE WINTERSON

The goal isn't more money. The goal is living life on your terms.

—CHRIS BOGAN

Live life on your own terms. Let everything good or bad, happy or sad make you strong and that's that.

—Deepa Rana

The world will always have an opinion about you, no matter what you may do. Be good to others, yet live life on your own terms.

—Author Unknown

Do more of what you love, less of what you tolerate and none of what you hate.

—John Assaraf

You'll learn, as you get older, that rules are made to be broken. Be bold enough to live life on your terms, and never, ever apologize for it. Go against the grain, refuse to conform, take the road less traveled instead of the well-beaten path. Laugh in the face of adversity, and leap before you look. Dance as though everybody is watching. March to the beat of your own drummer. And stubbornly refuse to fit in.

—Mandy Hale

Be bold enough to use your voice, brave enough to listen to your heart, and strong enough to live the life you've always imagined.

—Author Unknown

Your time is limited, so don't waste it living someone else's life. Don't be trapped by dogma—which is living with the results of other people's thinking.

Don't let the noise of others' opinions drown out your own inner voice. And most important, have the courage to follow your heart and intuition.

—Steve Jobs

It's time to take your life back from the people that are causing you pain and making you unhappy. Remember, this is your life and you are the author of your story. If you're stuck on the same page....just remember that at any moment you have the power to write a new chapter.

—Author Unknown

Being rich is living life on your own terms—according to your possibilities, not your limitations.

—Paul McKenna

The most important part of living life on your own terms and having it all is having faith and belief in yourself and in the intelligent power that created you.

—John Assaraf

Think for yourself. Trust your own intuition. Another's mind isn't walking your journey, you are.

—Scottie Waves

It doesn't make you a bad person to want to live your own life.

—Alexandra

You will find that people will always have opinions about your decisions. Don't take it personally, it's simply because they're not courageous enough to take action in their own lives. Be a leader in your life and pay no mind to those who lack the courage to dot the same in theirs.

—Dr. Steve Marboli

Being happy requires that you define your life in your own terms and then throw your whole heart into living your life to the fullest. In a way, happiness requires that you be perfectly selfish in order to develop yourself to a point where you can be unselfish for the rest of your life.

—Brian Tracy

The woman who follows the crowd will usually go no further than the crowd. The woman who walks alone is likely to find herself in places no one has ever been before.

—Albert Einstein

Start by making decisions about your life in a powerful way. No apologies for your decisions. Just stand by them 100%. And if you fall? Take 100% responsibility and get back up and dust yourself off, and keep going toward your dreams.

—Dr. Lara Fernandez

Of this be sure: You do not find the happy life…You make it.

—Thomas S. Monson

Don't bend; don't water it down; don't try to make it logical; don't edit your own soul according to the fashion. Rather, follow your most intense obsessions mercilessly.

—FRANZ KAFKA

The day you stop worrying will be the first day of your new life; anxiety takes you in circles, trust in yourself and become free.

—LEONE BROWN

I owe no explanations for my flaws. I don't have to justify my mistakes, my past, or my insecurities. I am growing and learning. Let me live.

—MAMA ZARA

Do something uncomfortable today. By stepping out of your box, you don't have to settle for what you are—you get to create who you want to become.

—HOWARD WALSTEIN

You are the master of your destiny. You can influence, direct and control your own environment. You can make your life what you want to be.

—NAPOLOEN HILL

Freedom is being you without anyone's permission.

—AUTHOR UNKNOWN

The Power of Owning Your Own Life

As a "Love Visionary," it is your responsibility to be the CEO of your own life! You need to own your life with leadership and love. You need to make the choices and decisions that are best for you and your goals, dreams, and VISION. You must "own" every area of your life! I'm talking about your fears, strengths, passions, weaknesses, addictions, and even your insecurities. You need to "own" all of it! When I say that you need to "OWN" it, what I really mean is that you need to acknowledge and accept all of your "SH*T"! You need to be fully aware of what your true weaknesses, fears, insecurities, and struggles are so that you can work on obliterating them with positive thoughts, emotions, beliefs, behaviors, and actions. As a "Student of Love," it is your job to work on eliminating the "SH*T" from your life and replacing it with "LOVE." You also need to devote a significant amount of time to working on developing your strengths, gifts, and talents. You have been greatly blessed by the Creator to have very special abilities that are unique to you. The various talents that you have were given to you with a specific purpose. That purpose is for you to utilize them. You need to gain precise clarity on what your strengths and gifts are, and then you need to focus on using them every day. When you live in a state of giving to others, you will be blessed abundantly.

The first rule for all "Love Visionaries" is that you must love yourself. You need to maintain self-care, self-confidence, self-respect, self-awareness, self-acceptance, and self-love. No matter what your past has been or what your current circumstances are…you must love yourself every day! When you live in this manner, you will be able to have a healthy and loving relationship with yourself. This is necessary in order for you to be a "Love Visionary" and lead a life of love that will enable you to give love, faith, and hope to others. Please pay attention to what I'm about to say to you: the most important relationship that you'll ever have in your life is the relationship that you have with yourself. In the process of learning how to passionately love yourself, your desire and ability to show love to others will significantly grow and intensify. When you truly begin living in a state of love, love becomes the fuel that ignites your life, your relationships, your passion, and your purpose. Love is the most powerful force in the universe. Are you ready to "own" LOVE? It's now time for you to fully commit to truly, madly, and deeply loving yourself! Your "Love Vision" journey is just beginning.

CHAPTER 9

The Power of Your Sixth Sense

WHEN YOU LOSE a sense…you gain a sense. Through my own personal experience of having vision loss, I have been enlightened to the body and mind's amazing ability to adapt in order to accommodate for the loss of one sense. I truly believe that when a person loses one of his or her senses, or if one sense is weakened, the body and mind automatically adapt, and the person's other senses become strengthened. In addition, I also believe that the person's intuition becomes extremely strengthened and heightened to perceive messages through an energy medium that is beyond our understanding. This powerful energy allows individuals to receive important messages through tapping into the mind, body, and soul connection.

One's sixth sense is ultimately the most powerful sense. It transcends time and space. This intense feeling of "knowing" and "sensing" transcends logic, analysis, and rational thought. I believe this is the opening of the heart that in turn deeply connects us to our most authentic selves, others, and the world. It allows us to be truly empathetic and compassionate so that we may feel things on a deeper level.

Everyone has the ability to access and utilize a sixth sense. In order to do so, you must clear your mind, open your heart, and create a sacred space of belief and faith. This sense of openness that you create within yourself will begin to expand your world, dissolve your self-imposed limitations, and allow yourself to connect to the Universe for divine guidance. It is a fact that there exists a world that is infinitely vast in comparison to the tangible world that we live in. Unfortunately, our society has only taught us to look outward for answers rather than learning how to access the unlimited and invaluable sources of information and knowledge that lie within our reach. As a result, most sixth senses have atrophied. It is time to "AWAKEN" your sixth sense so that you can begin living more passionately, purposefully, and boldly. Through accessing this sense, your choices and decisions will become more thoroughly grounded and informed. You will begin to sense and understand deeper meanings and possible outcomes. You will begin to have a faith that will change you and your world.

There are many ways that you can tune in and awaken your sixth sense. The process of incorporating this into your daily life will provide you with a divine guidance and wisdom that will help direct you to fulfill your destiny.

Exercises to Access Your Intuition

1. **Make it a priority to be fully present in your own life.** You must make the conscious decision and effort every day to be fully present in your life so that you can remain aware and awakened to all of the signs and subtle messages that the Universe is presenting to you. Don't allow your life to get so crazy and hectic that you feel as though you have no control. If your life becomes too chaotic and packed with input, you will become too busy to stop and acknowledge what your intuition is telling you. Your intuition is an extremely precious gift that has been given to you to help guide you and give you a sense of direction and purpose in your life. Learning to become fully present in your own life will allow you to follow your intuition and fulfill your destiny.

   Exercise: Make the commitment to live fully present in your daily life so that you can access and acknowledge the voice of your intuition.

2. **Pay attention to the vibes you're receiving.** Have you ever met someone and felt immediately uncomfortable? Have you had a sense of danger before there were any signs that something bad had happened? Have you ever felt like you should follow what your "gut instinct" is telling you to do? This could be anything such as the deep feelings that you have that you should quit your job, move, end a relationship, or get out of a current situation. Sometimes…your intuition will tell you things that you may not even be ready to hear, let alone acknowledge. You may even be worried about what others will think of you if you take action on these strong emotions. You may even feel foolish or silly for wanting to listen to these deep-rooted feelings. But don't ignore these signs! You need to listen to these important messages; they are vital signs to help guide you to take the appropriate actions in your life. They are there to protect and guide you on a path of purpose and passion.

Exercise: Quiet your mind, and remain committed to receiving the signs, messages, and signals that your intuition and the Universe are sending you.

3. **Search within yourself to find the answers.** If you're seeking answers and meaning in life, trying to make important decisions, or just needing creative solutions, you must turn inward. You must commit to connecting with your inner self, and ask the questions that are necessary to your subconscious mind. A lot of the important questions that are needed to help guide you in your life are contained within this book. Ask yourself these questions, and wait patiently; the answers will come to you. If the answers don't come immediately, keep asking yourself the questions. Rest assured, as your insights, memories, and the power of all of your senses will unite together to provide you direct guidance.

   Exercise: Commit to the continual process of searching within yourself for the answers that you're seeking.

4. **Let your dreams give insight.** While you sleep at night, your subconscious mind is completely free to process all of your innermost thoughts, feelings, emotions, and desires. This natural process that occurs can greatly help us by offering us insight into some of our biggest problems, concerns, fears, and important life events.

   Our dreams present us with "vivid" imagery, symbols, signs, and situations that many people believe are symbolic messages to help enlighten and direct us to our destined paths. I highly recommend that you do some research and reading on dream interpretation. In doing so, you will be able to reap the full benefits of all of the psychic support and guidance that your dreams can provide you.

   Exercise: Keep a dream journal, and make sure to write down your dreams as soon as you remember them. This will allow you to connect deeply to your intuition and subconscious mind.

5. **Spend time in nature.** Commit to spending ten or fifteen minutes in nature every day. This will allow you to develop a healthy habit that will help you get out of your conscious mind and more into an intuitive state. Our minds, bodies, and souls need nature in order to maintain our psychological, emotional, and physical well-being. So many people in today's society don't spend enough time in nature. They use their busy lifestyles and hectic schedules as their personal excuses for not having enough time. Being too busy…preoccupies their daily lives. They are unable to connect with all of the natural beauty that surrounds them. We must make it a priority to take a few minutes every day to allow ourselves to connect with nature. This is vital in order for us to live fully present in our lives and remain connected to ourselves, others, and the world.

   Exercise: Begin spending ten or fifteen minutes in nature every day. Make this one of your nonnegotiable "healthy habits." Enjoy this time by meditating in the beauty that surrounds you; let your mind be free. This practice will teach you how to become more attuned to the world around you and more receptive to the natural signs and messages that the Universe is sending to you on a daily basis.

6. **Let writing give you wisdom**. Keep a daily journal in which you write your innermost thoughts, feelings, emotions, desires, and dreams. Let this journal serve as your personal sacred space to freely express your most authentic self. This is your nonjudgment zone, where you will be able to gain clarity and clairvoyance through direct communication with yourself and the Universe. Openly expressing yourself will allow you to reclaim your voice. You will become empowered as you begin to speak your "authentic truth" out into the world. As you begin to communicate openly and fearlessly with yourself, others, and the world, miracles will happen.

   Exercise: Commit to writing in your journal every day. Your assignment is to write fearlessly from your soul. Embrace your inner voice, and unleash your innermost fears, desires, goals, and dreams. Let it flow….Expressing your authentic truth will change your life as you begin to take action on your deepest desires.

THE "RADICAL RULES" TO IGNITE YOUR INTUITION AND LIVE A LIFE OF PASSION

- **Rule One:** Let go of fear, judgment, preconceived notions, and your insecurities that you are not good enough, strong enough, smart enough, beautiful enough, etc.…

- **Rule Two:** Let go of your self-limiting and destructive beliefs, thoughts, emotions, and feelings that are holding you captive from living a life that you love.

- **Rule Three:** Embrace love, compassion, and empathy toward yourself, others, and the world every day.

- **Rule Four:** Exhibit courage, adventure, and risk by taking direct action on your goals every day.

- **Rule Five:** Explore your innermost desires, dreams, and passion by living boldly and fearlessly in the world.

- **Rule Six:** Be open to the unlimited possibilities and opportunities that the Universe will provide to you as you keep your heart and mind open to receive.

CHAPTER 10

Live Free or Die

HAVE YOU EVER felt as though you weren't living life to your fullest potential? Do you sometimes feel as if you're only going through the motions of life just to get by? Are you afraid to take action on your dreams and goals due to fear of the "unknown" and the potential risks that may result if you choose to live your life as you desire? Are you currently in an emotional, psychological, spiritual, or physical state of being (health and wellness) that you are unhappy and dissatisfied with? What about a job or relationship? If you answered yes to any of these questions, then it's time for you to wake up and begin living a life full of freedom! You only have one life to live! You deserve to make it your best life now! I'm talking about right now, in this present moment! You don't have time to waste! Life is meant for fully living in freedom so that you can live a life that you love.

When we let fear into our lives, it takes control over our mental, emotional, psychological, physical, and even financial states of being. Fear paralyzes us. Fear kills us from the inside out. It destroys our biggest dreams, goals, desires, hopes, and faith. The force of fear can throw us off course from our God-given path to fulfill our destinies.

I once was in a job that I greatly disliked. Each day I dreaded the monotonous routine of pure emptiness. Every day that I woke up and went to this job, I felt as though I was just going through the motions of life. I knew deep inside that I wasn't being true to myself or my dreams, goals, and desires. I had let fear take control over me and my life. Even though I so desperately wanted to quit my job every day that I walked into my office, I let the fear of losing a steady paycheck rule my life.

As I was walking into work one day, I noticed the state tagline on a New Hampshire license plate. It read "Live Free or Die." This was my wake-up call! I literally stopped walking and read it again: "Live Free or Die." Every day for the next few weeks, I couldn't ignore all of the New Hampshire license plates that I saw. I felt as though I began to see them everywhere!

That one little phrase "Live Free or Die" spoke deeply to my soul. I was at a pivotal point in my life. I felt as though I wasn't living in a state of freedom but was instead living in a state of fear. Although my deepest dreams, goals, desires, hopes, and faith were still inside of me...........I felt as though a part of me had died. Every day that I went through the motions of just "surviving" in a job that I desperately hated, I couldn't ignore the sadness of my soul. The "Live Free or Die" message on the New Hampshire license plate was my sign from the Universe! This was my personalized message from the Universe telling me that it was time to awaken my mind, body, and soul to begin living a life of FREEDOM!

It is our birthright as being children of the Universe to live lives of FREEDOM! We are meant to follow in the footsteps of our Creator.......by taking fearless action to implement and create that which is deep inside our souls. For we each are called for a higher purpose and plan, but we must be willing to hear our callings and respond by letting go of the fears in our lives. When we let fear into our lives, our charisma, faith, hope, and passion begin to die. It is time for us to ignite our "deepest passions" in order to awaken and bring back to life our dreams, goals, and desires so that we may fulfill our true callings and destinies. So.......how are you going to "reignite" your PASSIONS? The answer is inside of you! Only you know what you need to do in order to reclaim your freedom and start living the life you were destined for. Let your heart guide you; it will give you the answers that you need, and it will help direct you to take the appropriate steps that you need to take in order to create change in your life. Your heart is your compass, and it will direct the footsteps and choices of your life to your destined path.

Exercise: How to Awaken Your Soul

The following exercise is designed to help awaken your soul so that you can "reignite" the dreams, goals, and passion that reside inside of you…so that you can begin living in true freedom and fulfill your destiny. The following steps listed below will give you the guidance and direction that you need to start taking immediate action in your life so that you can create a life that you absolutely love! Get ready!!!! The steps below will require you to be deeply open, real, and honest with yourself, others, and the Universe.

- **Step One:** Utilize your personalized "Love List" that you designed for yourself from this book. Begin to incorporate as much of what you LOVE into your life so that you can reignite your passion and awaken your inner child.

- **Step Two:** UNLEASH your CREATIVITY in your life 365 Days a Year!

- **Step Three:** Get REAL with YOURSELF! Utilize your "Love Vision" journal to express your innermost thoughts, desires, goals, and dreams.

- **Step Four:** Get REAL with others! Begin speaking your "AUTHENTIC TRUTH" to others, and be honest in your relationships. Talk freely about your desires, goals, and dreams and how you're going to make them your reality!

- **Step Five:** Start taking immediate action on creating what's inside of you…even if you don't know where to begin. Start by taking baby steps. Research what you need to know in order to create your desires.

- **Step Six:** Live BOLDLY, FEARLESSLY, and FULLY in the PRESENT MOMENT!

- **Step Seven:** Dream big, and take action on all of that which is inside of you. Do not play small! You were created to CREATE! Every day, take action to make your desires, goals, and dreams your reality!

Life Begins When You Start Living OUTSIDE of Your "Comfort Zone"

Life truly begins when you start living outside of your "comfort zone." When you're willing and ready to venture, explore, and live in the realm of the "unknown," your world will begin to expand. I believe that when you step outside of your "comfort zone," you are stepping into a new a new dimension. This dimension will allow you to experience a life beyond your wildest dreams, a life in which anything is possible. Get comfortable being uncomfortable! Get confident being uncertain about the unknown, and firmly believe in yourself! Don't give up when you are faced with difficult circumstances, people, and situations. Pushing though uncertainty and the "unknown" will challenge you and enable you to grow.

Expansion happens in your life when you surrender to the Universe and release all of the fears that are holding you captive from living fully present in your own life on a daily basis. I'm talking about all of your fears…..anything that is holding you back mentally, emotionally, psychologically, physically, or spiritually from living your best life now. You know many of your darkest and deepest fears. Some you may not even have the courage to face. These fears….all of them…the big ones and the small ones….are holding you captive and are forcing you to live in your "comfort zone" every single day of your life. They are stealing from you the joy, peace, happiness, love, success, financial abundance, freedom, and blessings that you should be receiving as being a child of God.

But….there is good news! There is actually wonderful news! You have the power to reclaim your birthright and cast out all of the fears in your life that are keeping you imprisoned from living your purpose and fulfilling your destiny! Every day when you wake up, you are given the gift of free will to choose how you want to live your life.

You have two options. You can choose to either live your life based in fear or in freedom. When you choose to live in fear and base your decisions in fear, you are choosing to live in the safety of your "comfort zone." But there is no safety here! For when you choose to live in this zone, you are not challenging yourself, your goals, desires, or dreams. You are choosing to just "survive" and not "thrive." This is the zone in which your passion for life will die. This is where you will begin imposing self-limiting thoughts and beliefs into your daily life that will ultimately shape the way in which you view the world. As a result, your reality will be created from your innermost emotions, feelings, thoughts, and beliefs that are deeply rooted in fear. This fear-based perception will not allow you to live your best life now! This is why it is so important for you to wake up every day and to choose to live your life in freedom.

When you choose to consciously live your life in freedom, you are making the decision every day to choose positive and self-supporting emotions, feelings, thoughts, and beliefs that will allow you to create a life that you love. When you choose freedom over fear, you are choosing the power of love. Love is the most powerful life force and energy in the Universe. Love conquers all fears! Love is the creator of miracles! Choosing freedom and love is the beginning of your life. When you start living in true freedom outside of your comfort zone ("the unknown"), massive miracles will begin to happen in your life. The Universe will bring to you the circumstances, people, resources, ideas, and opportunities that you need to fulfill your destiny. You will be given the strength, faith, courage, and passion to create a life that you love. This life of love will far surpass your comfort zone. So get ready! Now is the time to start living boldly, fearlessly, and passionately!

Exercise: Break Free from Living in Your "Comfort Zone"

The following exercise contains six steps that you can begin incorporating into your daily life in order to "BREAK FREE" from living in your comfort zone. These steps are not intended for the weak of heart. They require you to be bold, fearless, and passionate! Be open and honest with yourself when choosing the specific steps that you need to take in order to create change in your life. Don't be afraid….you must take RISKS in order to bear the REWARDS that you desire in your life

- **Step One: Dare!** You must commit to have a sense of adventure in your daily life! For when you "DARE," your sense of adventure will create a life beyond your wildest dreams. Dare to take unprecedented action toward creating a life that you love!

- **Step Two: Explore.** You must be willing to explore your goals and dreams and any opportunity that has the possibility to manifest your desires.

- **Step Three: Take risks.** You must be willing to take chances in your life! You need to be vulnerable to the "unknown" and firmly believe in yourself enough to take risks that will manifest your dreams.

- **Step Four: Sacrifice.** You must sacrifice certain momentary highs in life and work your "*SS OFF" in order to build your vision and leave behind a legacy that will last far beyond your lifetime. Sacrifice the "superficial" crap, and work on building your empire!

- **Step Five: Invest.** Invest in yourself to become the person you were destined to be! Choose positive and self-supporting thoughts, emotions, beliefs, and actions that will allow you to accomplish your dreams. You must invest in yourself! Period. End of story. This is a nonnegotiable. You must constantly invest in your mind, body, and soul in order to grow and align yourself with the people, circumstances, and opportunities that will allow you to create your vision.

- **Step Six: Create.** You must release your creativity and artistry in this world! Unleash your "Inner Child," and be fearless! Play, create, and live with passion every day! Dream big, and remember to work your "*SS OFF" in order to make your VISION your reality!

The Magical Five-Question Formula

Do you remember learning the "Five W-How Questions" way back in grade school? Your teacher taught this questioning formula to help you collect key information about your writing topics. You were instructed to answer the following questions: Who? What? Where? When? Why? How? These questions were the foundation to help you gather key information that was needed in order to tell a story.

Well, I'm here to tell you that this powerful question formula holds the keys to unlocking the answers to some of life's most important questions. They will also help you create your future story. I will use this magical question formula throughout *Love Vision* by applying its core fundamental principles through strategic questioning. Your honest answers to these questions will help you gain clarity on your identity, goals, desires, and vision. The key word here is "honest." You must dig deep within yourself, and let your heart be completely honest when you're answering these questions. Your ability to speak your truth, desires, and passion will enable you to begin creating a life that you love. I've listed below the Love Vision "Five W-How Questions" that are personalized just for you. Your answers to these questions will help you design a blueprint for your Love Vision journey so that you can live a life full of passion and purpose as you fulfill your destiny.

Exercise: The Love Vision "Five W – How Question's"

Clear your mind, open your heart, and be in the present moment as you read and answer the below questions. Take your time in answering these questions. Incorporate this questioning exercise into your daily life. For the more you ask yourself the below questions, the more you will become focused and committed to your life's purpose, passions, and vision. Once you gain clarity and are able to honestly answer the below questions, you will be able to stand firm in your identity, knowing who you are as a person and what your purpose on this earth is for. You will be able to live a life full of passion as you fulfill your destiny, leaving behind a legacy that only you could create.

1. Who are you?

2. What is your passion, purpose, vision, and plan for your life?

3. Where do you want your "Love Vision" journey to take you?

4. When are you going to start taking action and begin accomplishing your goals, creating your vision, and fulfilling your destiny?

5. Why do you want to accomplish your goals, create your desired vision, and live your dream life?

6. How are you going to accomplish your goals, create your vision, manifest your dreams, and fulfill your destiny?

CHAPTER 11

—⟨&⟩—

F*CK Your Fears, Fulfill Your Destiny

I GREW UP in a very religious household, where the "F" word was forbidden. It is the one word that I still can't say in front of my parents. Although…sometimes there's no other word that seems to hold as much power as the "F" BOMB! Especially when it comes to talking about your fears. I even contemplated whether or not I should share this message in *Love Vision*. After meditating on the message that I deeply felt I needed to share about the "F" BOMB….I grabbed my pen and wrote the new chapter headline "F*CK Your Fears, Fulfill Your Destiny."

After writing this down and reading it out loud, I no longer felt uncomfortable with my choice of verbiage. The "F" Bomb holds a certain power of intensity and meaning that no other word seems to possess. When you make the conscious decision to "F*CK" your fears, you aren't messing around. You're being extremely serious about "F*CKING" (killing/destroying) your fears so that you can fulfill your destiny. When you begin "F*CKING" your fears, miracles will begin manifesting in your life. Your life will begin to change as you step into your own power and begin thinking, speaking, believing, and living your "authentic truth."

Your "AUTHENTIC TRUTH" is the innate wisdom and knowledge that your soul possesses; it is the essence of your being. What's your "authentic truth"? Dig deep within your soul, and answer this question. Trust me….your mind, body, and soul know the answer. For each of us, our truest purpose becomes clear when we begin answering the deep questions of the meaning of life and then begin living boldly in accordance with what resonates with our soul. When we awaken our "authentic truth," it's as if we are turning on our inner lights and igniting our souls so that we can live fearlessly and be who we truly are.

Living in a state of profound authenticity requires you to be rooted in your deepest truths, values, and beliefs and being 100 percent committed to living a life that is a true reflection of them. It about being true to yourself on a daily basis—through your words, thoughts, beliefs, relationships, and actions. It's about making "self-love" your first priority. It means being willing to sacrifice any relationship, situation, circumstance, or limiting thoughts and beliefs that violate your "authentic truth." Once you start living fully in your "authentic truth," you will begin hearing the voice of your "inner knowing." You must commit to listening to this voice; it will provide you guidance for your daily choices and will direct you to the path that will allow you to fulfill your destiny.

WHEN IT COMES TO YOUR DREAMS, DON'T GIVE A SH*T ABOUT WHAT PEOPLE THINK!

OK…..I promise you…this is the last time that I'm going to use a "bad" word in *Love Vision*. But seriously…..You can't give a "SH*T" about what people think about you, your dreams, and the way in which you choose to live your life! You need to ask yourself the following questions:

1. Am I going to allow the opinions of others and the fear of what I think others may say about me deter me from living my dreams?

2. Do I value the opinions and words of others over my own "authentic truth"?

You need to get real with yourself and decide whose voice you're going to listen to. Will it be the voice of others? Or will you rely on the voice of your "authentic truth," which possesses the innate wisdom and knowledge to help direct you to fulfill your destiny? When you start not giving a "SH*T" about the opinions, thoughts, words, and criticism of others, you will start fully living and begin taking unprecedented action toward your dreams. It's now time to give a "SH*T" about YOU, YOUR GOALS, DESIRES, and DREAMS! You only have one life to live, and it's not the life of how others may think you need to live. It's the life that you were born to live—a life completely free of fear, a life full of abundance, peace, joy, happiness, fulfillment, and LOVE! Freedom is calling you! Are you ready to answer and start building a life that you love? Now is the time! Not tomorrow, next week, next month, or next year. Right now in this moment is the time for you to commit to truly start living your life.

Bucket List

Do you have a Bucket List? If not, do you even know what a Bucket List is? A Bucket List is simply a list of all the goals you want to achieve, dreams you want to fulfill, and life experiences you desire to experience before you die. The term originally came from the 2007 American comedy-drama film called *The Bucket List*. The movie follows two terminally ill men—Carter and Edward (portrayed by Morgan Freeman and Jack Nicholson)—who escape from a cancer ward in order to head off on a road trip. They want to live out their list of to-dos before they "kick the bucket." This inspiring film has become a classic. It touches the hearts of many with its simple message of the importance of living life to the fullest through finding what brings you and others joy. I definitely recommend watching this film because it encourages you to make the most of every moment of your life…right up until your last breath.

Maintaining a Bucket List is helpful in reminding you of what's really important to you in your life and how you can act on your desires to achieve your goals and dreams. It's different from a Goal List because it's not strictly centered on one specific area.

A Bucket List opens up the context for you to put forth into the Universe everything and anything you've ever wanted to achieve or manifest. It extends to you a complete sense of freedom in setting all of the goals that you truly desire, no matter how big, random, or small they may be. In a way, a Bucket List allows you to plan ahead all of the highlights you desire to experience for the rest of your life. The purpose of creating a Bucket List is to maximize every moment of your existence and to ensure that you're living your life to the fullest. It's a strategic "to-do" list of all the things that you want to achieve and experience during your time here on earth. It helps us from wasting our time on meaningless activities and keeps our focus on the things in life that will truly fulfill us and bring us joy.

A Bucket List is a brilliant, vibrant, energizing, and inspiring strategy to incorporate into your life. For in keeping a Bucket List, you're guaranteed to gain significant clarity and focus on what it is that you truly desire to experience, achieve, and live out in this lifetime. Your personal Bucket List is priceless. Period, end of story. It's a complete no-brainer! It's a genius and creative plan to help you stay focused, motivated, inspired, and committed to making your dreams come true! It kind of puts you into "Wonder Woman" or "Superman" mode, in which you gain superhuman powers that keep you laser focused on achieving, accomplishing, and manifesting. This is where you will enter the vortex of living your life to the fullest. It is in this vortex of fearlessness that creativity, passion, and adventure will fuel your life so that you can kick your fears to the curb while you live freely, boldly, and courageously.

This got me thinking....If a Bucket List contains this much power, why wouldn't you create a focused Bucket List every year? In doing this, you would be able to accelerate your ability to accomplish your dreams every year by super-charging your focus, passion, and dedication. Your annual Bucket List would be your to-do list of every single goal, desire, and dream that you want to manifest that year.

So, I've decided, my dear "Love Visionary," that you were destined to create an annual "Love Vision" Bucket List every year. You're meant to live 365 days a year in "Wonder Woman" or "Superman" mode! You deserve to exert your superhuman powers every day of your life! You are meant to live in the vortex of unlimited possibilities so that you can create your VISION.

Make the conscious decision to commit to making a "Love Vision" Bucket List (LV Bucket List) each and every year! So....are you wondering what the requirements of a "Love Vision" Bucket List are? Well, you should be. An "LV" Bucket List is not your typical Bucket List! The items that you put on your list can be whatever your heart desires. They only requirement is that they must align with your VISION, PURPOSE, and PASSION. Your goal with all of the items on this list is to achieve, accomplish, create, see, feel, and experience all of them in the upcoming year. Your annual "LV" Bucket List will serve as your catalyst to help you take bigger risks and massive action so that you can "LIVE" your wildest dreams, desires, and goals!

CREATING YOUR "LOVE VISION" BUCKET LIST

If you desire to live your biggest and wildest dreams, you must be willing to commit to doing the BIG and WILD steps that will allow you to manifest your desires—every day. Are you ready? It's time for you to clear your mind and to dig deep down into your soul to gain clarity on what dreams you truly desire to "LIVE OUT LOUD" this year. I highly recommend picking five to ten of your dream goals to put on your LV Bucket List each year. Choose the goals that you are most passionate about! This will give you the fuel and focus to either do, accomplish, achieve, create, experience, or live out your biggest desires!

It's very important for you not to limit yourself when choosing your five to ten "LV" Bucket List items each year. You need to remove all of your fears and the self-imposed negative thoughts, emotions, and beliefs that are holding you back from living your life to the fullest. For in creating your "LV" Bucket List, you are required to list your biggest goals, desires, and dreams so that you can work all year at making them your reality! A "LV" Bucket List will stop you from procrastinating and saying "I'll do it next year!" It will get you in the habit of daily taking BIG RISKS so that you can reap BIG REWARS! You must be willing to constantly take risks in your life if you want to reap massive rewards! Taking risks will grant you priceless opportunities for immense growth, change, success, and happiness in your life. Living as a "risk-taker" will ensure that you live your life to the fullest by allowing you to live in a state of the "now" so that you can be fully present and take immediate action in your order to create, accomplish, and experience your wildest dreams!

If you never "try," you can never "do"! If you're never brave enough to spread your wings, you never will be able to fly! My dear "Love Visionary," you are destined to soar to heights that you never even dreamed were possible! It is time for you to truly "awaken" and to live your life fully alive in the present moment so that you can LIVE! It is time for you to start living—Fully, Fearlessly, and Free! You only have one life to live here on this earth. Today's the day to start truly living! RISK reaps "REWARDS" and a RADICAL lifestyle! You weren't created to play small. You were destined to play outside of the box so that you can create a life that you absolutely love: a life that is luscious, luxurious, and limitless!

Exercise: "Love Vision" Bucket List

List your top five-to-ten "LOVE VISION" BUCKET LIST items that you want to manifest and "LIVE OUT" this year. Don't just write down the first few things that come to your mind. Really give yourself time on this exercise to meditate on what your heart truly desires to live out this year. You only have one life to live, and this isn't a dress rehearsal. If you want to live an outrageous life…you must commit to taking outrageous action on a daily basis in order to create with the Universe and manifest your desires. You must be clear, concise, and courageous! Be as detailed as possible so that you can literally feel, taste, hear, smell, and see your "LV" goals becoming your current reality. The more descriptive you get in writing your goals, the more "alive" you make them become! The more "alive" you make your goals…the more "alive" you become in taking unprecedented action toward achieving them!

After you finish writing your top five-to-ten "LV" Bucket List Goals down…there's one more step that you need to complete. This step is the most important part! Wondering what it is? Well, you did a fabulous job at picking five to ten outrageous life goals to live out this year, so now…you need to map out next to each "LV" goal the outrageous plan, strategy, and action steps that will enable you to live out your dreams this year! As with the first step of this exercise…be extremely clear, concise, and courageous! The more "alive" you make your "LV" Bucket list goals…the more "alive" the Universe becomes at creating with you to help you manifest your dreams!

My Personal "LOVE VISION" BUCKET LIST

1. Secure a publishing contract for *Love Vision* with a major publishing company in order to share my message of "Love Vision" with the world

2. Get interviewed by the *New York Times* on "Love Vision"

3. *Love Vision* becomes a *New York Times* best seller

4. *Love Vision* BOOK TOUR

5. STOMP OUT BULLYING: Get funding to donate one million copies of *Love Vision* to "STOMP OUT BULLYING"—the leading national bullying and cyber-bullying prevention organization for kids and teens

6. Speak at a TEDx Event and share my story about "Love Vision"

7. Host a "Love Vision" radio show

8. Get interviewed on the following talk shows in order to share my message of "Love Vision" with the world: *Super Soul Sunday with Oprah Winfrey, The Today Show, Good Morning America, The View, The Talk, Ellen, Dr. Oz,* and *The Tonight Show* on NBC

9. Meet Katy Perry, who has deeply inspired me with her positive and uplifting music. Share my story with her about why I wrote *Love Vision* and ask her if she would write a song specifically about living with perseverance, passion, and purpose so that you can fulfill your destiny. (I know that this "LV" Bucket List Goal

is outrageous!!! But so is Katy Perry, and I truly believe that her song would be able to touch the lives of many...both young and old.)

10. Launch the weekly "Love Vision Membership" that will inspire "Love Visionaries" around the world

I have one last question for you before I leave you with some fabulous "WORDS OF WISDOM." The question is....Are you scared to write down your biggest and wildest dreams? Why???? Really think about this one! I just shared with you my biggest, wildest, and outrageous dreams and goals. Did you laugh at them? I sure hope not! But even if you did....it doesn't matter. The Universe doesn't care about the opinions of what others may think or say in regards to your goals, dreams, and life. The Universe only cares about where you place your attention, efforts, and action. For the Universe responds to those who are "alive" and living a life full of perseverance, passion, and purposeful action. Your dreams are your dreams! You are 100 percent entitled to dream as big, bold, and fearless as you desire! You're called as "Love Visionary" to live a life that you love. But don't fret, my child; your dreams are not in selfish vain! Your dreams have the immense power to touch, heal, motivate, inspire, and help the lives of many.

I'd like to leave you with a little inspiration to help motivate you to write your "LV" Bucket List. Hay House Publishing is one of the world's leading publishing companies for self-help, inspirational, and transformational books. Just a few months ago there was a motivational conference called "I CAN DO IT" that was going to be held in Ft. Lauderdale, Florida. I was extremely ecstatic when I found out that this conference was coming up and that it was only a little over an hour of a drive from where I live. Then the bad news came. I looked at my calendar and saw that I was scheduled to work all weekend. I was so bummed! I had high hopes of attending this seminar; my soul was desperately in need of teaching and inspiration.

At this time, I was working on writing *Love Vision*, and more than anything, I needed big-time motivation. As the days passed, I realize that the "I CAN DO IT" conference was coming up in a week. I began to hear a little voice in my mind that kept saying "YOU CAN DO IT. Just buy your ticket online and go!" I kept hearing this voice over and over.

It was two days before the conference, and I gave into this voice. I somehow managed to get out of working the Sunday event that I had been scheduled for. This gave me the opportunity to attend the conference on the last day of the event. That little voice inside of me kept encouraging me, saying "YOU CAN DO IT" and "YOU NEED THIS!"

Boy, am I ever glad that I had the courage and faith to listen to that voice inside of me! Through adhering to my inner guidance, I was able to "live out" a number of my lifetime "LOVE VISION" Bucket List goals on that Sunday. I was given the amazing opportunity to meet and talk to four of my favorite authors and spiritual leaders: Kris Carr, Dr. Christine Northrup, Davidji, and Mastin Kipp. The interactions that I had with these spiritual activists and my time spent at the "I CAN DO IT" conference far fulfilled my wildest dreams! I was given words of guidance, inspiration, and motivation that helped me continue my journey of writing and publishing *Love Vision*. Was it worth it? It was one of the best decisions that I've ever made in my life! For when you follow your heart, passion, and purpose you are destined to manifest your dreams.

Words of Wisdom on Living Life to the Fullest

Every man dies—Not every man lives.

—WILLIAM ROSS

The only people who fear death are those with regrets.

—AUTHOR UNKNOWN

Enjoy the little things in life, for one day you may look back and realize they were the big things.

—ROBERT BREAULT

All life is an experiment. The more experiments you make the better.

—RALPH WALDO EMERSON

Life is a game, play it; Life is a challenge, Meet it; Life is an opportunity, Capture it.

—UNKNOWN

The saddest summary of a life contains three descriptions: could have, might have, and should have.

—LOUIS E. BOONE

There'll be two dates on your tombstone and all your friends will read 'em but all that's gonna matter is that little dash between 'em.

—KEVIN WELCH

Twenty years from now you will be more disappointed by the things you didn't do than by the things you did.

—MARK TWAIN

Cherish your yesterdays, dream your tomorrows and live your todays.

—ANONYMOUS

Quit hanging on to the handrails…Let go. Surrender. Go for the ride of your life. Do it every day.

—MELODY BEATTIE

Be bold and mighty forces will come to your aid. In the past, whenever I had fallen short in almost any undertaking, it was seldom because I had tried and failed. It was because I had let fear of failure stop me from trying at all.

—ARTHUR GORDON

One way to get the most out of life is to look upon it as an adventure.

—WILLIAM FEATHER

Every day, it's important to ask and answer these questions: "What's good in my life?" and "What needs to be done?"

—NATHANIEL BRANDEN

A life without cause is a life without effect.

—BARBARELLA

There is only one success, to be able to spend your life in your own way.

—CHRISTOPHER MORLEY

Don't wait. Make memories today. Celebrate your life.

—UNKNOWN

Life has no limitations, except the ones you make.

—Les Brown

Life is a great big canvas, and you should throw all the paint on it you can.

—Danny Kaye

Don't be afraid your life will end; be afraid that it will never begin.

—Grace Hansen

You only live once, but if you do it right, once is enough.

—Joe Lewis

Somebody should tell us, right at the start of our lives, that we are dying. Then we might live life to the limit, every minute of every day. Do it! I say. Whatever you want to do, do it now! There are only so many tomorrows.

—Pope Paul VI

I don't wait for the calendar to figure out when I should live life.

—Gene Simmons

The purpose of life, after all, is to live it, to taste experience to the utmost, to reach out eagerly and without fear for newer and richer experience.

—Eleanor Roosevelt

It is not the years in your life but the life in your years that counts.

—ADLAI STEVENSON

Your Personal "Love Vision" Bucket List

CHAPTER 12

A Student of Love

NOW THAT YOU'VE made the decision to be a "Love Visionary," you've consciously chosen to become a lifelong "Student of Love." A "Student of Love" is a "Love Visionary" who is dedicated and committed to building and living a life that he or she loves. The Universe is your classroom. The people who come into your life—your family, friends, acquaintances, work colleagues, strangers, and even your enemies—are your greatest teachers. They have been placed into your life to teach you valuable lessons so that you can grow. These pivotal lessons are actually blessings in disguise; they will change you. They will make you a stronger person. They will alter your perceptions and change your state of heart. They will teach you how to become more compassionate, empathetic, gracious, supporting, forgiving, and loving.

Sometimes the circumstances, situations, and people in our lives cause us such pain, sorrow, anger, and grief that we become overwhelmed by our emotional state and begin to feel incapable of handling the situation. Our lives can become extremely difficult when we are living in this state of fear. But this is when we are truly given the opportunity to have faith and believe in something far greater than ourselves. This is the time in which we must choose to cast out the fears in our lives and to ignite our faith on fire! For when we "ignite hope" in our lives, our faith in ourselves, others, and the Universe will catch on "FIRE"! This fire has the power to burn through all of the difficult circumstances and situations that you will face in your life. "FAITH on FIRE" produces miracles.

You were placed on this earth to both learn and teach. As being a "Love Visionary"— "Student of Love"—it is your job to instill value in yourself, others, and the world. Through dedicating yourself to living a life of love, you are committed to letting LOVE be your guide. With each life experience, you learn more about yourself. You begin to see how your reactions and patterns affect yourself, others, and the world around you. You learn how to take charge and break free from the negative thoughts, emotions, beliefs, and actions that use to be a part of your daily life. Remember......"LOVE" is your best inner teacher. It will guide you throughout your life and give you the strength to fulfill your lifelong "Love Visionary" journey.

Invest in Yourself

In being a "Student of Love," every day you should invest in yourself: your mind, body, and soul. You need to research and learn about all of the people, places, things, ideas, and actions that will enable you to fulfill your vision. You need to become an "expert" and "specialist" on how you will create your dreams. Just as a builder needs a blueprint for constructing a home or building, so too do you need a blueprint for creating the life that you desire. You need to invest your time in building a very detailed blueprint, one that will outline for you the various steps that you need to take on a daily basis in order to give you the structure and guidance that you will need to make steady progress in building your vision. You will need to get crystal clear on what your goals are and then develop a strategy and plan that will allow you to accomplish them.

Next, you will need to dedicate yourself to investing in your vision. You will need to fill your life with the appropriate people, opportunities, learning experiences, and resources that will help you with your construction process. Choosing to invest in yourself, your dreams, and vision comes with a price. This will require for you to make many sacrifices. You will have to learn how to prioritize your life so that you can focus your time, energy and resources on investing and building your vision.

The Requirements of Being a "Student of Love"

Merriam-Webster gives the following definition of a "student": (1) a scholar, learner; and (2) one who studies: an attentive and systematic observer. In being a "Student of Love," it is a requirement that you are willing and ready to "show up" every day in your own life, present and ready to learn. This is a nonnegotiable. You must "show up" every day and be fully present so that you are aware of the people, situations, circumstances, and opportunities in your life—as well as your thoughts, emotions and beliefs. You need to "tune in" to your mind, body, and soul and truly connect with who you are. You must be able to answer the following question: "Who am I"? The answer to this question is your true identity as a "Student of Love." For in knowing who you are, you will be able to stay grounded in your authentic truth and committed to your purpose of living a life of love on a daily basis. This will enable you to learn and grow because you will be fully engaged in living your life in the present moment.

The second requirement of being a "Student of Love" is that you must stay inspired and motivated in your own life. If you don't stay inspired, your passion will die. Without passion, you will be unable to live a life of love. Passion is the "magical ingredient" that will allow you to stay focused, committed, and dedicated to a accomplishing your goals, creating your dreams, and fulfilling your destiny. Losing your passion will throw you off course to fulfilling your destiny. When your passion dies, your ability to remain true to yourself, goals, desires, and dreams weakens. You become susceptible to living a life in "survival mode" as opposed to living a life full of passion in which you would be able to live in "thriving mode."

Survive or thrive? How do you want to live your life? It's up to you to decide, as you're the one who holds the power to determining how you will live your life. No one else is going to be your personal cheerleader. You need to become the personal cheerleader of your own life. You need to motivate, encourage, and inspire yourself every day to live a life full of passion. You must align your words, thoughts, emotions, feelings, and beliefs about yourself, others, and the world to your vision. Surround yourself with positive people, circumstances, situations, and opportunities that will allow you to learn, grow, and flourish. Fill your life with the people, places, ideas, and things that you love! The things that excite you are not random. They're connected to your purpose. Follow these things. They will lead you step-by-step on the path that you're destined for.

If you are having trouble in gaining clarity on what you're true passions are, dig deep within your soul, and ask yourself the following questions. What do you feel you were born to do? What excites and motivates you? What do you strongly believe in? What do you feel your lifelong purpose is? What makes you happy? What makes you want to get out of bed in the morning? What do you love? What do you value? What is meaningful to you? What is rewarding to you? How can I give love to others? What fulfills you?

Your answers to these questions are your passions. Follow them. Love will not lead you astray. As a "Student of Love" it is your job to be a lifelong learner of love. Every day you need to strive to learn, teach, and grow from a place of love. In doing so, you will be able to live a life of love and fulfill your destiny.

Your Gifts and Talents

As a "Student of Love," it your responsibility to discover what your gifts and talents are and to freely give them to others. Your talents will enable you to creatively give love: "Each one should use whatever gift he has received to serve others, faithfully administering God's grace in its various forms." (1 Pet. 4:10 NIV) For in giving these gifts with a grateful heart and not expecting anything in return, you will be blessed. In return, you will receive far more back from what you give. I'm not referring to material abundance. I'm speaking directly about the priceless abundance that comes from giving—the joy, peace, happiness, and contentment that your heart will receive from giving to others.

Everyone is given a unique set of gifts and talents in order to help fulfill a God-given destiny. We each possess special abilities, personalities, and experiences that make us who we individually are as people. Life is not about using these gifts just to work, make money, pay bills, save money, retire, and die. You are meant for so much more than that! God has given you your unique gifts and talents to help you create a life that you love, one that will touch the lives of many. God has given you these gifts and talents to use. They're kind of like muscles. If you use them, they will grow. If you don't, they will lose their strength. Choose to use them wisely; if you do, the Universe will bless you.

Inspirational Words about Giving

The purpose of life is to discover your gift. The work of life is to develop it. The meaning of life is to give your gift away.

—DAVID VISCOTT

It's not how much we give but how much love we put into giving.

—MOTHER TERESA

We make a living by what we get. We make a life by what we give.

—WINSTON S. CHURCHILL

You give but little when you give of your possessions. It is when you give of yourself that you truly give.

—KAHLIL GIBRAN, *THE PROPHET*

A kind gesture can reach a wound that only compassion can heal.

—STEVE MARABOLI, *LIFE, THE TRUTH, AND BEING FREE*

I slept and I dreamed that life is all joy. I woke and I saw that life is all service. I served and I saw that service is joy.

—KAHLIL GIBRAN

Learn to light a candle in the darkest moments of someone's life. Be the light that helps others see; it is what gives life its deepest significance.

—ROY T. BENNETT, *THE LIGHT IN THE HEART*

Get Your "Love Vision" On!

Get ready to put on your "Love Vision" glasses to learn how to view and transform your physical, emotional, spiritual, and psychological pain into a passion and love for yourself, your life, and others. Getting your "Love Vision" on is the most effective way to start transforming your life from the inside out. "Love Vision" is the most potent and powerful narcotic available.

Society's solutions or alternatives such as drugs, alcohol, sex, lies, etc…will only temporarily numb the pain and lead one on a downward spiral. The search for truth and contentment will only lead to one's self-destruction. We could write a book on the alluring alternatives that the "SSS" offers. Use your past personal experiences and imagination to elaborate on the endless pollution of dangerous options.

"Love Vision" is not like society's attempts to dilute or numb pain. "Love Vision" is a radical change of one's perspective and mind-set to begin a healthy healing process from the inside. Love is the answer. It's that simple. All we as human beings need is love.

"Love Vision" will enable you to wake up and see that anything and everything is possible. You need to have your "Love Vision" on in order to truly connect with your inherent truth. One of my favorite meditations is by the world-renowned Deepak Chopra in his book, *The Secret of Love*. Please take a few minutes to clear your mind and meditate on some of the powerful and inspiring words that Deepak reveals in his meditation.

> The secret of love is self-love in the ultimate sense. Self-love does not refer to the love of your ego-self or your personality. Self-love is to be in the knowing that you are completely loved and completely loveable. And then the world will mirror that knowing. Love is meant to heal. Love is meant to renew. Love is meant to make us safe. Love is meant to inspire us with its power. Love is meant to remove all doubts. Love is meant to oust all fear. Love is meant to unveil immortality. Love is meant to bring peace. Love is meant to harmonize our differences. Love is meant to bring us closer to God.

The best news is that "Love Vision" is absolutely free. It is available to all of humanity and society. No credit card is required. It can't be purchased in a store or online. It cannot be given to you from a friend, family member, colleague, celebrity, or even your lover. "Love Vision" is available to you free of cost at any given moment in your life. It is available for you at all times. I will repeat…"Love Vision" can't be bought. It's a choice. It is a daily choice. It is an hourly choice. It is a minute-by-minute choice. "Love Vision" is the innate ability to alter one's perspective and mind-set at any given moment of one's life.

It's a moment-by-moment choice to choose to view life with love over fear. It is necessary that we live in the present moment and that we are present within ourselves in order to choose love over fear. Fear manifests itself in many forms. Many of us have experienced fear in all of its nasty, paralyzing, painful, and agonizing forms. The result of giving in and believing your fears leads only to a lack of hope, faith, strength, and courage. Fear gives birth to worry, depression, sadness, jealousy, resentment, anger…The list is endless.

"Our Deepest Fear" by Marianne Williamson

The following is an excerpt from one of my favorite authors and spiritual teachers, Marianne Williamson. This passage is from her best-selling book, *A Return to Love: Reflections on the Principles of a Course in Miracles*:

> Our deepest fear is not that we are inadequate. Our deepest fear is that we are powerful beyond measure. It is our light, not our darkness that most frightens us. We ask ourselves, Who am I to be brilliant, gorgeous, talented, fabulous? Actually, who are you *not* to be? You are a child of God. Your playing small does not serve the world. There is nothing enlightened about shrinking so that other people won't feel insecure around you. We are all meant to shine, as children do. We were born to make manifest the glory of God that is within us. It's not just in some of us; it's in everyone. And as we let our own light shine, we unconsciously give other people permission to do the same. As we are liberated from our own fear, our presence automatically liberates others.

The breakthrough of our generation is going to start now with "Love Vision"! This new truth will awaken our society to emerge as spiritual leaders, thought provokers, entrepreneurs, and love activists. With this new awareness and mind-set, we will be enlightened and empowered to inspire ourselves and others to live a life full of love!

Love Is the Frame

The most powerful feature that "Love Vision" offers is its solid and indestructible frame. The frame of all "Love Vision" glasses is love. The frame of love will never change; it will save the day. Once you have decided to accept and claim "Love Vision," your life will change forever. We all come from different backgrounds, belief systems, cultures, and religions, I believe that the following scripture is applicable to all of humanity:

> Love is patient, love is kind. It does not envy, it does not boast, it is not proud. It does not dishonor others, it is not self-seeking, it is not easily angered, it keeps no record of wrongs. Love does not delight in evil but rejoices with the truth. It always protects, always trusts, always hopes, always perseveres. Love endures all. (1 Cor. 13:4-7 NIV)

Your Lenses Are Interchangeable

Now it's time to reveal the most unique and creative feature of "Love Vision." You're now aware that the frame of love will always remain constant. The astounding revelation is that your lenses are interchangeable. You have the power to change your frame's lenses at any given moment. This phenomenal ability will enable you to change your fear-based belief system and build a belief system based on love.

With this new knowledge of "Love Vision" you now have the power to change your perspective at any given moment in your life. Your new perception will directly affect how you view yourself, your life, others, and the world. It is a fact that one's perception shapes one's reality. You have the power to shape and create your own personal reality and the reality of others at any given moment.

The various perceptions (the "lenses" that you choose to insert in your "Love Vision" glasses) that you choose daily will drastically alter your innermost thoughts and beliefs. As a result, your new belief systems and inherent truth will guide you to live your life with passion and purpose. Through creating new intentions, choices, and actions, your mind will be empowered and strengthened as your life begins to expand.

Your Values Are Your Lenses

Your personal values are your interchangeable lenses. Many people define the word "value" differently. In this case, we are referring to values as one's belief system of the qualities, characteristics, and states of being that one believes are necessary, important, and desirable to have in their lives. One's personal values directly shape his or her self-awareness, choices, and actions. Personal values are implicitly related to choice; they guide our decisions by allowing our choices to be in alignment with our core values and beliefs.

Our values are developed early on in our lives. The majority of our values we have adopted from our culture, family, friends, religion, background, and society at large. Most people even believe that these values are completely resistant to change.

NEWS FLASH!!!!

I'm super excited to share with you some shocking information that our society has been keeping secret. You have the power to choose your own personal values! No one or nothing can influence your ability and innate power to choose how you want to live your life. Since personal values evolve from circumstances within the external world, this gives us the incredible power to change them at any given moment. These interchangeable "values" (what I refer to as "lenses" in this book) will drastically alter your perception of the world.

Now that you are fully aware of the truth, you can make the decision to dispose of the old, foggy, and dirty glasses that you have been wearing. You need to remove the frame and lenses of fear and negativity that the "SSS" has so graciously given to you. It's now time for you to get your "Love Vision" on!

"Love Vision" will allow you to view the world with the most precise clarity, granting you the creativity, confidence, and courage to live your life to the fullest. Although "Love Vision" is absolutely free and accessible at any given moment of your life, you must learn the secret of how to access it. The secret is in the process of self-identification. Once you decide and commit to live your life with "Love Vision," you must identify which value's "lenses" you want in your life. The value "lenses" that you choose will give you the opportunity to expand your life entirely. This is the beginning of expansion. Are you ready?

Self-Identification

Exercise: Self Identification- Identifying your "Authentic Truth"

The self-identification exercise that you're about to undertake is going to require a great amount of soul searching. Get ready to dig deep within yourself; you now need to summon the courage to be honest with yourself as you begin the process of identifying how you truly desire to live your life.

This exercise will enable you to expand your mind to the unlimited possibilities that you have on a daily basis to alter your perception, thoughts, choices and actions in order to accomplish your goals. Through the process of identifying who you are, who you would like to become, and how you desire to live your life…you will begin to create a VISION for your life. This VISION will be built entirely on what you love. As a result, you will have the freedom to start living a life that you absolutely love.

CREATE YOUR PERSONAL VALUES LIST

Listed below you will find a very extensive list of values "lenses" that you need to review.

- **Step One:** Come prepared to this assignment with an open mind and heart.

- **Step Two:** Take your time to thoroughly review and study the listed values.

- **Step Three**: Grab your pen, and begin to circle all of the values that resonate with you. Circle the ones that you think describe you, things you want more of in your life, and the values that you want to build your life upon. Include all values that you believe will serve you, your goals, and your overall vision of how you want to live your life.

- **Step Four**: Stay focused, and be serious with yourself when reviewing the values that you are considering incorporating into your life. Keep reading and contemplating over which values you truly feel resonate with your goals, desires, and

VISION. Continue circling all values that are a "fit" for you and your life until you reach the end of the list,

- **Step Five**: Review all of the values that you circled.

- **Step Six**: Utilize your built-in "Love Vision" journal to prioritize your new set of values in their order of importance, significance, and power in your life.

- **Step Seven**: Begin to incorporate these values into your day-to-day life.

- **Step Eight**: Meditate on your values.

- **Step Nine**: Connect to your values.

- **Step Ten**: Believe in your values.

- **Step Eleven**: Live your values.

List of Values

Listed below is a very extensive list of values "lenses" for you to freely choose from to insert into your "Love Vision" frames and to incorporate into your life. I know what you're thinking...This list is ridiculously long!!! Long it is...but it's unlimited in its potential for the new possibilities, thoughts, feelings, beliefs, and actions that you will gain from its unique power.

Take your time when reviewing this list. You can even take a break from reviewing this list and come back to it whenever you feel you are ready. Creating a new personal-value list for how you want to live your life on a daily basis is a very emotional and intense job. This process is the beginning of changing your life's direction so that you can live your ultimate destiny with passion and purpose. Get ready to be inspired!

Abundance	Acceptance	Accessibility
Accomplishment	Accuracy	Achievement
Acknowledgment	Activeness	Adaptability
Adoration	Adroitness	Adventure
Affection	Affluence	Aggressiveness
Agility	Alertness	Altruism
Ambition	Amusement	Anticipation
Appreciation	Approachability	Articulateness
Assertiveness	Assurance	Attentiveness
Attractiveness	Audacity	Availability
Awareness	Awe	Balance
Beauty	Being the best	Belonging
Benevolence	Bliss	Boldness
Bravery	Brilliance	Buoyancy
Calmness	Camaraderie	Candor
Capability	Care	Carefulness
Celebrity	Certainty	Challenge
Charity	Charm	Chastity
Cheerfulness	Clarity	Cleanliness
Clear-mindedness	Cleverness	Closeness
Comfort	Commitment	Compassion
Completion	Composure	Concentration
Confidence	Conformity	Congruency
Connection	Consciousness	Consistency
Contentment	Continuity	Contribution
Control	Conviction	Conviviality
Coolness	Cooperation	Cordiality
Correctness	Courage	Courtesy
Craftiness	Creativity	Credibility
Cunning	Curiosity	Daring
Decisiveness	Decorum	Deference
Delight	Dependability	Depth
Desire	Determination	Devotion
Devoutness	Dexterity	Dignity
Diligence	Direction	Directness
Discipline	Discovery	Discretion
Diversity	Dominance	Dreaming
Drive	Duty	Dynamism

Eagerness	Economy	Ecstasy
Education	Effectiveness	Efficiency
Elation	Elegance	Empathy
Encouragement	Endurance	Energy
Enjoyment	Entertainment	Enthusiasm
Excellence	Excitement	Exhilaration
Expectancy	Expediency	Experience
Expertise	Exploration	Expressiveness
Extravagance	Extroversion	Exuberance
Fairness	Faith	Fame
Family	Fascination	Fashion
Fearlessness	Ferocity	Fidelity
Fierceness	Financial independence	Firmness
Fitness	Flexibility	Flow
Fluency	Focus	Fortitude
Frankness	Freedom	Friendliness
Frugality	Fun	Gallantry
Generosity	Gentility	Giving
Grace	Gratitude	Gregariousness
Growth	Guidance	Happiness
Harmony	Health	Heart
Helpfulness	Heroism	Holiness
Honesty	Honor	Hopefulness
Hospitality	Humility	Humor
Hygiene	Imagination	Impact
Impartiality	Independence	Industry
Ingenuity	Inquisitiveness	Insightfulness
Inspiration	Integrity	Intelligence
Intensity	Intimacy	Intrepidness
Introversion	Intuition	Intuitiveness
Inventiveness	Investing	Joy
Judiciousness	Justice	Keenness
Kindness	Knowledge	Leadership

Learning	Liberation	Liberty
Liveliness	Logic	Longevity
Love	Loyalty	Majesty
Making a difference	Mastery	Maturity
Meekness	Mellowness	Meticulousness
Mindfulness	Modesty	Motivation
Mysteriousness	Neatness	Nerve
Obedience	Open-mindedness	Openness
Optimism	Order	Organization
Originality	Outlandishness	Outrageousness
Passion	Peace	Perceptiveness
Perfection	Perkiness	Perseverance
Persistence	Persuasiveness	Philanthropy
Piety	Playfulness	Pleasantness
Pleasure	Poise	Polish
Popularity	Potency	Power
Practicality	Pragmatism	Precision
Preparedness	Presence	Privacy
Proactivity	Professionalism	Prosperity
Prudence	Punctuality	Purity
Realism	Reason	Reasonableness
Recognition	Recreation	Refinement
Reflection	Relaxation	Reliability
Religiousness	Resilience	Resolution
Resolve	Resourcefulness	Respect
Rest	Restraint	Reverence
Richness	Rigor	Sacredness
Sacrifice	Sagacity	Saintliness
Sanguinity	Satisfaction	Security
Self-control	Selflessness	Self-reliance
Sensitivity	Sensuality	Serenity

Service	Sexuality	Sharing
Shrewdness	Significance	Silence
Silliness	Simplicity	Sincerity
Skilfulness	Solidarity	Solitude
Soundness	Speed	Spirit
Spirituality	Spontaneity	Spunk
Stability	Stealth	Stillness
Strength	Structure	Success
Support	Supremacy	Surprise
Sympathy	Synergy	Teamwork
Temperance	Thankfulness	Thoroughness
Thoughtfulness	Thrift	Tidiness
Timeliness	Traditionalism	Tranquility
Transcendence	Trust	Trustworthiness
Truth	Understanding	Unflappability
Uniqueness	Unity	Usefulness
Utility	Valor	Variety
Victory	Vigor	Virtue
Vision	Vitality	Vivacity
Warmth	Watchfulness	Wealth
Wilfulness	Willingness	Winning
Wisdom	Wittiness	Wonder
Youthfulness	Zeal	

After completing the self-identification exercise, you should feel really empowered in knowing that you have the power to choose exactly how you want to live your life. You're now fully aware that when you combine your personal values with the supporting thoughts, beliefs, choices and actions you will be able to accomplish your goals and live your desired VISION.

This exercise is one that you should do daily. Think of it as drinking water. You need to drink water every day to stay healthy and hydrated. The more water you drink, the more hydrated your body is. This exercise will replenish and hydrate your soul. It will truly quench your thirst!

Through incorporating this exercise into your daily life and meditating, connecting, and believing in its vital significance…you will begin living your values on a daily basis. Now that you're truly enlightened to the importance and worth of your personal values ("lenses"), your perspective on your life is changed forever! This new perspective grants you the wisdom and knowledge to know that you have the power to create a life full of love.

The Visibility of "Love Vision" Glasses and Lenses

Vogue, Prada, Dolce & Gabana, DKNY, Ralph Lauren, Tiffany & Co., Oakley, Ray Ban, Coach, and Bulgari are some of the top eye-wear brands desired by the masses. These brands offer their clients the highest fashion and style, all the while providing them an enhanced clarity and precision to view the world.

We all can admit that at one point in time we have said to someone, "I love your glasses!" "Cool shades!" or, "Where did you get those awesome sunglasses?" This was a simple action of awareness, acknowledgement, and admiration. Contemplating this…made me start to think on a completely different level. What if "Love Vision" glasses and lenses were visible for everyone in our world to see?

How would this change our world? It would awaken all of our society to the power that "Love Vision" offers to all of humanity. It would reveal who was living a life of love and who was living a life full of fear, pain, and hopelessness. The HOT-RED FRAMES of "Love Vision" worn by every "Love Visionary" would be completely visible for the world to see.

This new reality would give us the ability to see those less fortunate souls who have chosen to wear the "SSS" glasses, adopted from our superficial society. With this new "sixth sense" of sight, we would be enlightened to the truth. We would begin to understand that the "SSS" glasses and lenses that are worn by the masses are truly blinders.

The "SSS" blinders are ultimately captivating, imprisoning, and destroying our society. They're the death of our generation. These blinders are built with an indestructible "ego-centric" frame. The "lenses" of these blinders are leading their owners—"prisoners"—on a downward-spiral search to fill the void of love that is missing from their lives.

CHAPTER 13

It's Time to Ignite a "LOVE VISION" Generation!

NOW THAT WE are aware of our innate ability to live a life of "Love Vision," it's time to use our light to ignite our generation on fire! Let us be fully present, dedicated, and committed to our true identity. The time is here. It is our destiny and calling to be as flames amid the darkness and to live fearlessly with "Love Vision" that is transparent for the world to see.

Let us choose to be the light in the darkness. Let our bright effervescent flames of love shun the darkness. Let us aspire to spread the message of "Love Vision" to all. Let us share this life-altering message to our friends, family, colleagues, acquaintances, and the strangers we meet.

Remember, we are all interconnected. "Love Vision" is the answer that our generation has been so long awaiting. Love, strength, freedom, hope, and healing are available to all. Restoration is here! Let us collectively unite to accept, embrace, and embark on the journey of "Love Vision." Let us inspire, motivate, and encourage one another to daily live with perseverance, passion, and purpose. Let our HOT-RED FRAMES of "Love Vision" be transparent for all to see.

"Love Vision" vs. "SSS" Blinders

Now that you are enlightened to the life-changing power that you possess with "Love Vision," take a few moments to meditate on the positive benefits and power that it will yield. Following the benefits of freedom that you're about to read, you will also be given the traits and negative power that the "SSS" blinders possess. Meditate on the following traits, attributes, emotions, and states of being that both of these "visions" gift.

"LOVE VISION"

Self-love
Self-acceptance
Self-analysis
Self-assurance
Self-awareness
Self-belief
Self-care
Self-confidence
Self-consciousness
Self-control
Self-disciplined
Self-dignity
Self-determination
Self-educated
Self-esteem
Self-examination
Self-excitement
Self-healing

Self-help
Self-hope
Self-faith
Self-joy
Self-inspiration
Self-motivation
Self-peace
Self-mastery
Selfless
Self-nourishment
Self-knowing
Self-realization
Self-reflecting
Self-reliant
Self-respect
Self-restraint
Self-sacrificing
Self-satisfaction
Self-secure
Self-starter
Self-support
Self-will
Strong self-worth

The "SSS" Blinders

Self-abandoned
Self-ashamed
Self-absorption
Self-abuse

Self-addiction
Self-broken
Self-compare
Self-conceit
Self-guilt
Self-confused
Self-critical
Self-damaged
Self-depressed
Self-distressed
Self-deceit
Self-denial
Self-death
Self-dependent
Self-depricating
Self-despair
Self-detached
Self-destructing
Self-disbelief
Self-disrespect
Self-doubt
Self-flattery
Self-hate
Self-harm
Self-hopelessness
Self-hypocritical
Self-judgment
Self-neglect
Self-pity
Self-pleasure

Self-righteous
Self-sabotage
Self-seeking
Self-serving
Selfish
Self-torment
Self-oppressed

Disidentify

THE PROCESS OF DETOXIFICATION

Your mind, body, and soul are now in a very healthy state of being after completing the self-identification exercise and reflecting on the life-changing power of "Love Vision." You have made the commitment to live a healthier, happier, and more fulfilling life. This is super exciting!

Now that you've decided to fill your life with only good things, you must remove all of the bad. It sounds simple...but detoxifying is far from that. The first step in detoxification is to identify the bad and then to choose to disidentify with it. It is one of the most challenging and difficult things that we need to do in our lives.

This is not a one-week detox cleanse. You must disidentify and detox on a daily basis in order to live a healthy life.

In preparation for this exercise, you need to fully mentally prepare yourself of its deep significance and importance. You need to make the mental association that your values, habits, thoughts, and beliefs are directly comparable to food. I know what you're thinking...have I gone BANANAS?!?!? The answer is YES!!!! We need to directly relate the process of self-identification and dis-identification to food. When I refer to food... I'm really trying to visually create the mental picture for you that your values, habits, thoughts, and beliefs are your nutrition. Your nutrition is what fuels your life.

Everyone has the daily choice to fill their diet full of healthy and nourishing foods. Many people are very conscious of their diet and its direct correlation on their physical, mental, and even emotional states of being. Most of our society is even quite obsessed with the body and body image, living lives dedicated to maintaining very healthy diets to achieve desired physical outcomes. This isn't a bad thing...it just surprises me. Why, you might ask? I'll tell you why. I'm actually astounded that people who are so conscious of what they put in their body are totally ignorant to what they feed their mind and soul on a daily basis.

If you really begin to meditate on this truth, you will begin to "awaken." Many people fill their bodies with the healthiest foods, but they feed their minds and souls with utter crap! They continue striving to maintain a healthy and strong physique; all the while their minds and souls are malnourished. This malnourishment will ultimately lead to a very unhealthy, unhappy, and unfulfilled soul. You're now about to embark on the process of dis-identifying and detoxing. Grab a pen—it's time to detox, baby!

Exercise: Disidentify- An Exercise of Detoxification

Create Your Personal Detox List

- **Step One**: Be present and alert.

- **Step Two**: Write all of the values that you presently hold that do not serve you, your goals, and your VISION.

- **Step Three**: Write all of the thoughts and feelings you have that do not serve you, your goals, and your VISION.

- **Step Four**: Write all of the choices that you have made and are thinking of making that do not serve you, your goals, and your VISION.

- **Step Five**: Write all of the temptations that you struggle with that do not serve you, your goals, and your VISION.

- **Step Six**: Write all of the beliefs that do not serve you, your goals, and your VISION.

- **Step Seven**: Meditate on your personal detox list.

- **Step Eight**: Awaken your mind, body, and soul to their life-threatening powers.

- **Step Nine**: Decide and commit to daily detoxify your life of these harmful substances.

- **Step Ten**: You have two options:

1. Tear up your personal detox list to signify your detoxification and removal of its power over your life, or

2. Keep this list in your journal for reference...sort of like a JUNK FOOD LIST. This gives you the opportunity to continue to reflect back on your old diet and nutrition. You can review this JUNK FOOD LIST at any given time to remind yourself of its harmful and negative side effects.

- **Step Eleven**: Repeat this exercise when needed.

- **Step Twelve**: Refuel, recharge, replenish, and renew your mind, body, and soul daily with your values list.

- **Step Thirteen**: Live with purpose and passion.

Your Personal Detox List

Laying the Foundation…Get Ready to Use Your Shovel!

It's Time to Build, Baby!!!!

You now are on the start of building your own personal foundation. Just as a house requires a firmly laid foundation and a precise construction and design plan, your life requires the same. The remaining exercises and techniques in this book will help you to build a life that you love. Get ready to build….You have a lot of work ahead of you!

It's time to find your soul-searching shovel and summon up the strength and courage to start digging deep within yourself in order to complete the following exercises. Within your heart lie your lifelong goals, desires, and dreams. It's finally time to access the "secret key" that will unlock your full potential, motivation, inspiration, and ability to make your dreams a reality.

If you don't have a specific vision for your life, then you can't live it. Without having, knowing, and being committed to a specific vision, you are literally just conforming to life as it happens. WAKE UP! You need to get off of autopilot and start living the life that you've always dreamed of!

You are the only one on this planet earth who knows exactly what you truly desire in this world and how you want to live your life. Now that you have identified your core values, it's time to build your own personal goals and vision. You must dedicate your mind, body, and soul to the lifelong creative process of building and living your vision. Choose to be committed to yourself, your values, your goals, and your vision on a daily basis. You will be required to love, move, act, design, and inspire yourself in order to create. This is the beginning of "your life."

The following questions in the next exercise (YOLO, or "YOU ONLY LIVE ONCE") are all directed to you and to you alone. Grab your journal and a pen. You don't have any time to waste. You only live once. You're about to undertake the most valuable Q&A interview in your life. The person asking the questions is you and the person answering the questions is you. The following rules apply in order to achieve the maximum results for your life.

Rules of the YOLO Exercise

1. You must be as honest as possible.

2. You must be as accurate as possible.

3. You must be extremely detailed.

4. You must hold nothing back.

5. You must be willing to fearlessly unleash your innermost thoughts and desires.

Exercise: YOLO Exercise

(You Only Live Once)

What does your dream life look like?

How would you live your dream life?

How does living your dream life feel?

Describe in detail your perfect life....

Where would you live?

Where would you work?

What career/business dreams would you be pursuing?

Who would you be friends with?

What type of relationships would you have in your life (with friends, family members, coworkers, clients, and romantic relationships)?

What would the nature of these relationships be like?

What type of activities and fun adventures would you do with these various people?

How would it feel to have these types of relationships in your life?

What type of activities, exercises, and hobbies would you be passionately pursing?

How would you feel being involved in multiple activities that you truly loved?

How would you positively contribute to this world (volunteering, getting involved in charitable organizations, etc.)?

How would it feel to know that you're making a difference in this world?

What lifelong dreams have you given up on?

Why did you give up on pursuing these dreams?

What does your ideal body look like?

How does this ideal body state feel?

What does your ideal health state look like?

How does it feel to have this ideal health state?

What does your dream career/business life look like?

How does having this dream career/business life feel?

What does your ideal social life look like?

How does it feel to have this social life?

What does your desired spiritual life look like?

How does it feel to be living this desired spiritual life?

Describe your dream financial situation?

What does it feel like to have this financial life?

What do you really, really, really want?

What is it that you love to do?

What truly motivates and inspires you?

What makes you want to be creative?

What are your strengths, gifts, and talents?

What are your skills?

What skills and talents do you want to passionately pursue?

What interest you?

What do you want to learn?

Where do you want to travel?

What makes you truly happy?

What makes you smile?

What do you do best?

What truly fulfills you?

What is something that you always have wanted to be extraordinary at?

What would you like to do more of in your life?

What new activities and adventures do you desire to explore?

What engages you?

What strengthens you?

What empowers you?

What awakens you?

What energizes you?

What refreshes you?

What enlightens you?

What expands your mind?

What encourages you?

What do you passionately believe in?

What makes you come alive?

What ignites your soul?

What excites you and gets you out of bed each morning?

What are you living for?

Who are you living for?

What are you waiting for in order to start living the life that you've always dreamed of?

Exercises: Writing Your VISION & Creating Your Vision Board

WRITING YOUR VISION EXERCISE

Now it's time to deeply reflect on your answers to the above questions and to write a thorough description of your desired VISION in your "Love Vision" journal. Your VISION is the ultimate dream that you have for your life. It consists of your lifelong goals (relationship, career, body, health, financial, spiritual, social life, etc.) as well as your personal values. Use the answers from the above Q&A section to ignite your creativity. Make sure that you allow yourself plenty of time to complete this part of the exercise.

You must abide to the following five rules when writing your VISION.

1. Be as detailed as possible.

2. Be as creative as possible. (Use your IMAGINATION.)

3. Be as honest as possible.

4. You must describe fully your deepest dreams and goals.

5. You must be fearlessly free, open, and expressive in order to reveal your deepest desires.

Write Your VISION

Use the following "Love Vision" journal space to write out your VISION. This is the most important exercise in "Love Vision." Open your mind, body, and soul...Let your mind and heart do the writing.

Your VISION

The Importance of Your "Brain and Heart" in Your VISION Equation

John Assaraf is one of my favorite authors and motivational speakers. The following excerpt, taken from his article "The Power of Having a Vision," has greatly affected my perception on the importance and structure of my own personal vision for my life. Please take a moment to read his words of wisdom. Be prepared to be enlightened.

The latest research proves that when we're fully engaged and emotionalized in our clear vision, we emit a frequency from our brain and heart that penetrates and permeates all space and time, and brings forth to us everything that's in resonance with the image we're holding.

The frequency we emit is our personal electromagnetic frequency. Just like a radio station that sends out a signal, we send ours out based on our dominating thoughts at a conscious and subconscious level.

Just imagine the way an apple seed attracts the nutrients it needs from the soil to grow its roots, and then once it sprouts above the ground the sun adds its magic and food through photosynthesis. Then, low and behold...the seed becomes an apple tree.

You too, will attract exactly what you need to realize your dreams when you really start to believe and feel your vision becoming a reality. It's the clear and consistent vibration of your vision that brings forth your needs. You provide the seed, the universe provides the resources.

Therefore, you must now make your "new vision" inside your brain more real than the current results in your outside world. Then, and only then, will the universe begin to present its riches to you in the most convenient and efficient ways possible. **Your clear vision is your seed.** Choose it wisely and precisely, and riches beyond your imagination in every area of your life shall be yours.

DESIGNING YOUR PERSONAL VISION BOARD

You're the architect of your own life. Within you remains the power to create, design, and build the life that you truly desire. Your love, passion, motivation, inspiration and creativity are the driving forces of your destiny. Through designing a personal vision for your life, you will have a solid construction plan that will help you identify the required "building blocks" (your goals and personal values) that you will need in order to build this vision.

You will need the following materials before you begin the VISION BOARD EXERCISE: a large piece of poster board (you can choose any color that you desire), scissors, magazines, a sharpie pen, and a glue stick. Your written vision and your answers from the YOLO Q&A will give you the mental framework for the creative aspect of this project.

VISION-BOARD EXERCISE

- **Step One:** Begin flipping through your magazines. I highly suggest gathering a variety of different publications such as fashion, design, home, lifestyle, business, relationships, and so on. Grab your scissors and begin cutting all of the images: places, people, art, beautiful architecture, words, phrases, and so on. It is your mission to cut the images of anything, anyone, or anywhere that inspires you! You will need enough artwork to fill your entire piece of construction paper.

- **Step Two:** Let your creativity and imagination take control! Now it's time to break out the glue stick and begin the process of making your vision a visual reality. Paste your artwork as you desire. This is your VISION BOARD and yours alone. Be fearless and free as you design your masterpiece. Keep in mind that this beautiful VISION will remain yours forever. Your VISION BOARD will serve as a visual reminder of your most personal goals, dreams, hopes, and desires. It is built with the sole purpose to motivate and inspire you when needed and to serve as a blueprint for your dreams.

Your vision will serve as your guiding star and will direct you in creating your personal goals. Once you have clearly identified your goals, you will be able to begin planning the necessary actions that are required to yield your desired results. Your daily goals, choices, and actions serve as the fundamental building blocks of the ultimate vision that you have designed for your life. You must be diligent and choose to plan wisely the appropriate choices and actions that will enable your vision to become your reality.

Goal setting is a process of self-discovery that will help you create new opportunities for ongoing learning, growth, and success. It will give you the ability to design actions that will ultimately lead you to fulfill your goals. It is very focused on the exploration of the unlimited ideas, options, and solutions that are available to you. You need to realize that you have unlimited choices and unlimited possibilities. The power remains in your hands. The question is, how are you going to utilize and apply this power?

While it is true that without a vision the people will perish, it is doubly true that without action the people and their vision perish, as well.

—JOHNNETTA BETSCH COLE

CHAPTER 14

Goal Training 101

IT LITERALLY AMAZES me that most schools don't have specific classes to teach goal setting and vision creation. With the increased rate of school bullying and teen pregnancies, along with drug, alcohol, and tobacco use, you would think that schools would start to implement such educational programs. There needs to be a "Love Vision" educational training available for children and people of any age to learn the fundamental principles, skills, and mind-sets that will empower them to make smart choices for their lives.

"Love Vision" education would fully equip our future generation to be love activists, social and visionary entrepreneurs, and world changers. Can we present this educational request to our president? I think we should! The following section is dedicated to the life-altering process and application of goal-setting. Prepare yourself for Goal Training 101!

Exercise: Developing Your Personal Goals

Grab your "Love Vision" journal! It's time to create and develop your personal goals, which ultimately shape your vision and life. After reviewing the goal requirements below, grab your journal and begin writing your goals. Rely on your mind, body, and soul to inspire you to write the desires, dreams, and goals of your heart.

Open your journal and read your written VISION prior to completing this goal-development exercise. Read it twice. Close your eyes, and meditate on your vision for several minutes. Generate within yourself the positive feeling of your VISION and the life that you desire to build. Let your mind lead you from this place to start creating your individual goals. Your goals are the building blocks of your VISION. Your goals will help you design a master plan for a life that is full of passion, purpose, and power.

The following are the key requirements that all of your goals need to possess in order for you to reach goal attainment.

1. The goal must be aligned with your Vision.

2. The goal must be tangible (concrete, solid, real).

3. The goal must be measurable.

4. The goal must be phrased in the positive.

5. The goal must be phrased in the past or present tense, such as "I AM" or "I HAVE." (Stating your goals as if they've already happened puts your mind in a very positive state so that your actions align accordingly.)

6. You must believe 100 percent in your goals

7. You must be 100 percent dedicated to accomplishing your goals and be fully committed to completing all necessary actions to achieve success.

In order to help you start brainstorming and writing your goals effortlessly…Answer the following questions in your "Love Vision" journal first, and then start a "GOAL-SETTING" section in your journal where you can begin to freely write your goals on a daily, weekly, monthly, and yearly basis.

The below questions are designed specifically to help you write clear and concise goals. The clearer you're able to imagine your goals being attained, the faster and easier it will be to manifest them.

Goal Setting

QUESTIONS TO HELP YOU START WRITING YOUR
PERSONAL AND PROFESSIONAL GOALS:

1. What does your ideal life look like?

2. What course does your ideal day run?

3. What are three things that would drastically improve the quality of your life?

4. If you had all the money that you needed, what would your life look like?

5. What does success look like for you?

6. What does success feel like for you?

7. What does happiness look like for you?

8. What does happiness feel like for you?

9. What are you currently working towards creating?

10. What is your lifelong dream?

11. What do you feel that you are called to do as part of your destiny?

12. What kind of legacy do you want to leave behind, once you leave this earth?

13. What GOALS can be derived from how you envision your ideal life?

14. What dream or goal have you given up on?

15. What goal have you put aside because you didn't think the timing was right?

16. How much do you buy into this GOAL?

17. How is this GOAL aligned with who or what you want to be?

18. What is the first "BIG STEP" (translation- "GOAL") that you need to take in order to get you closer to your "VISION"?

19. What are 5 additional steps ("ACTIONS") that you can take that will help you achieve your GOAL?

After answering all of the above questions, you must ask yourself the following question: What's the first "BIG STEP" (goal) that you need to take that will enable you to get closer to attaining your desired goal(s)? After you write your first "BIG STEP" (goal), you just need to continue adding the additional "STEPS"—"ACTIONS" that you need to take in order to accomplish your goals and manifest your desires.

IMPORTANT FACTS TO KNOW ABOUT THE "GOAL-SETTING" PROCESS

- Goal setting is an emotional process.

- People choose goals based on how they think the attainment of that goal will make them feel (happier, more content, secure, etc…).

- Therefore, discovering what matters most to you ("Your Values") is the most important step in creating your goals.

- Goal setting is based on your ideal VISION of your life.

- Thus, when setting goals…your VISION is ultimately what drives the whole goal-setting process

IMPORTANT TIPS FOR ACHIEVING YOUR GOALS

- Having confidence is a very important part of goal attainment.

- Acting as if the goal has already been completed will put your mind in a positive state and will allow for your body to acclimate toward doing so.

- What do you have to lose by acting and thinking positively?

- Put your goals to the goal test: How committed are you on a scale of one to ten to this goal? Who will keep you accountable toward achieving this goal?

Clarifying the Need for GOALS (Life Change)

The questions you must answer to make sure you're ready to commit to your goals:

1. If nothing changes in your life, what will that feel like to you?

2. What are the advantages of changing?

3. What are the disadvantages of changing?

4. What are the disadvantages of not changing?

5. What do you think would help make this new life possible?

The Importance of Creating an "ACTION PLAN"

Designing your own personal "ACTION PLAN" is necessary in order for you to reach your goals and to manifest your VISION. Just as the popular Nike sports brand encourages us….You need to "JUST DO IT"!!!!!

Your "ACTION PLAN" is created based upon your goals, once you have identified the need for change in your life. You need to work on creating an "ACTION PLAN" every day in order to make progress toward your goals. This creative personal method will involve multiple actions from you physically, mentally, and emotionally. You will be required to maintain an optimistic attitude and invest your time, energy, and efforts in order to manifest your desires.

For each goal that you're working toward reaching…you need to ask yourself what the first step is to reach this goal. You then need to work on creating multiple "ACTION STEPS" that will allow you to reach your goal.

Exercise: Questions for Designing an "Action Plan"

1. What is the best thing that you can do this week that will help you attain this goal?

2. What activities are you willing to do to get you closer to your goal?

3. What do you need to change to attain this goal?

4. What are you willing to complete this year? In the next 6 months? 3 months? This month? This week? Today? *** Set Action Steps for every DAY ***

5. So, what are your options?

6. What options call your heart?

7. How can you move forward?

Exercise: Building Your "Support Network"

Now that you have a clear VISION for your life and know exactly what it is that you want to create, you need to make sure that you have a "support network" of people in your life. These individuals will be there to help support, motivate, and love you along your journey. They will give you the extra strength that you need to stay focused on your goals, and they can also hold you accountable for the actions that you have committed to. These people can be your friends, family members, mentors, colleagues, etc...The below questions are designed to help you build your "support network."

1. Who offers you the most support in your life right now?

2. Who are the key people in your life and what do they provide for you?

3. Who or what is holding you back most right now?

4. What do you think that you can do about this?

5. What resources can you draw on to help you achieve your goals and dreams?

6. Who do you think would be a great mentor for you in offering advice, support, and guidance towards helping you achieve your goals?

7. Who can you ask to be part of your "support system" to help keep you accountable, motivated, and inspired?

8. Who can you ask for help, support, and guidance?

CHAPTER 15

Analogies and Symbolism

I ABSOLUTELY LOVE analogies! For those of you who are curious about what an analogy is, it's simply the literary comparison of two things to reveal their related similarity. A very common analogy that most of us have heard is from the classic movie *Forrest Gump*. Forrest expresses his thoughts on life by saying "My momma always said life was like a box of chocolates. You never know what you're gonna get." This famous quote has great meaning and is a great analogy for life.

Analogies allow you to paint a very detailed and creative picture in people's minds when you're trying to explain something. You will actually find that I tend to use them a lot in *Love Vision,* for the sole purpose to help you reframe your mind. If we can become familiar with certain analogies and the great significance that they contain, we can utilize that knowledge and reframe the picture that we currently hold in our minds. Reframing is the process of using positive and powerful information to help you reframe your mind-set to view things in a different perspective. Reframing is the ability that you have every moment of your life with "Love Vision."

I actually have a few favorite analogies that I love to use to help explain the significance and importance of one's goals and vision. Below you will find my three favorites. I will then proceed to explain the analogies in further detail so that you will be able to utilize them to reframe your mind-set and to apply them to your goal-setting and vision-creation process.

You can utilize the below analogies to create your own personal goal-setting and vision-creation exercises. Make sure to record these exercises in your "Love Vision" journal. Creating your own unique exercises and reframing techniques will get your mind in creation mode. This mode will take you wherever you desire! Get ready to create!

1. Your life is like a house.

2. Your vision and goals are like a puzzle.

3. Your goals are like the "secret keys" to opening the doors of your dream life.

4. Your vision is like your roadmap in life.

YOUR LIFE IS LIKE A HOUSE

Your life is like a house. You reside in your house as you reside in your own life. The vision that you have for your life is similar to a house. The vision and house both require firm foundations, strong building blocks, structure, and stability in order to maintain their presence. These key requirements of construction help one to endure the storms of life and maintain their places of residency without being shaken.

The vision that you create for your life is your house. The goals that you set are like the various rooms in the house. Think of the different types of rooms…the living room, dining room, kitchen, bedroom, family room, playroom, patio, garage, guest room, bathroom, and storage room. Each room serves a specific purpose and gives the house a sense of organization and structure, just as your goals do for your life.

Each room provides its own energy based on its design and décor. You have the creative power to decorate your home and all the rooms contained within however you desire. The style options are endless. This creative principle applies directly to your own life, goals, and vision. You have the innate ability to design and furnish your life in any way that you desire.

You're the only one who can create the style, substance, and structure. The possibilities are unlimited. You're a "Love Vision" designer. Your job is an interior and exterior decorator. Your interior work (your thoughts, beliefs, feelings, and mind-set) will produce the exterior décor in your life.

YOUR VISION AND GOALS ARE LIKE A PUZZLE

Wikipedia defines a puzzle as the following:

> A **puzzle** is a problem or enigma that tests the ingenuity of the solver. In a basic puzzle, one is intended to put together pieces in a logical way in order to come up with the desired solution. Puzzles are often contrived as a form of entertainment, but they can also stem from serious mathematical or logistical problems. Solutions to puzzles may require recognizing patterns and creating a particular order.

This is so relatable to how life is! Your life is exactly like a puzzle because we are all faced with problems and tests throughout our own personal journeys of trying to put the pieces of our lives together. The vision that we create and work to build is our desired masterpiece "puzzle," and it is the most beautiful piece of art that we will ever create in our lives.

It is vital that we identify the appropriate "puzzle pieces" (the various goals, thoughts, beliefs, feelings, and actions) that are required to start building our destinies. It is then a matter of accessing and utilizing our "Love Vision" to help guide us in putting the appropriate pieces together in order to successfully build our own masterpiece puzzle.

Through vision creation and clear goal setting, we will be able to implement a strategic puzzle-building strategy that will help us put together the pieces of our lives'. Puzzles provide much entertainment along the way... get ready to build your puzzle! The fun is just beginning!

YOUR GOALS ARE LIKE THE "SECRET KEYS" TO OPENING THE DOORS OF YOUR DREAMS

Merriam-Webster defines the word "key" as "a means of gaining or preventing entrance, possession, or control. A key is something that gives an explanation or identification or provides a solution." I believe that these two definitions hold a great deal of symbolism and truth to our lives if we can relate them to our goals. In essence, our goals are like the "secret keys" to opening the doors of our dream lives.

We have the freedom to create unlimited "keys" (goals) in our own lives in order to gain entrance, possession, or control of our own personal desires. These goals help us to explain and identify our dreams in order to provide us with a solid plan and solution. The only thing that is required of us is to create, access, and utilize our own personal "keys" (goals) so that we can open the doors to our destinies. Have you created your own unique set of destiny keys?

YOUR VISION IS LIKE YOUR ROAD MAP IN LIFE

A road map is defined as "a detailed plan to guide progress toward a goal" (*Merriam-Webster*). This definition of a road map can be directly compared to the importance of the personal vision that you create for your life. It is a known rule of thumb that if you're going to go on a road trip, you better bring along a road map. This road map will provide you with direction in your journeys so that you can reach your destinations and not get lost. Think about this for a minute…If it is standard procedure to carry a road map in your vehicle while venturing into unknown territory, wouldn't it make complete sense to do the same preparation for your own life?

The vision that you create for your life will serve as your detailed plan or so-called "road map." It will give you guidance in progressing toward the various goals that you have set for your life. The numerous goals that you set and focus on achieving are directly comparable to the various travel destinations that you have highlighted on your "road map." Your life is a journey. You can travel anywhere and everywhere. In order to reach all of your desired destinations, you must remember the following four rules.

The Personal "Road Map" Rules for Life

1. You must plan exactly where you want to go; all desired destinations must be clearly outlined.

2. You must have a "road map" (your VISION) with you at all times during your journey.

3. You must set clear goals (ACTION-STEPS) on how you're going to get to your various destinations.

4. You must be excited to drive the road ahead and be prepared for unexpected "road blocks."

5. You must enjoy the ride!!!

Symbolism

The Power of Bamboo

I recently asked my mentor if he could give me some words of wisdom to meditate on. I was in deep need of motivation to help me maintain the strength to continue my soul-expressing journey of writing *Love Vision*. After some silence, he looked me directly in the eyes and said, "You must learn to be like bamboo. You need to be flexible, yet strong…so that you can bend without breaking."

After hearing him say these words…It was as though an electric bolt of energy surged through my body. I knew deep inside of me that what he just said contained an immense amount of wisdom and truth. I was speechless—yet extremely intrigued.

My curiosity led me on a deep quest to learn more about the symbolism of bamboo. Through my research, I soon discovered that the symbolism of the bamboo plant runs deep and offers valuable lessons for life. The practical, aesthetic, and spiritual significance of bamboo is deeply embedded in both Japanese and Chinese culture. To the Chinese people, bamboo is the symbolization of virtue. It reflects people's souls and emotions. It is a symbol for longevity, as it always maintains green shoots—as well as strength and grace—because it bends readily but doesn't break easily. Bamboo symbolizes strength, acceptance of the natural flow, and openness to wisdom in emptiness. It is also symbolic of commitment to continuous growth and living a simple and straightforward life.

Through my intense research efforts online, I came across the following beautiful description of the bamboo plant:

> Bamboo is flexible, bending with the wind but never breaking, capable of adapting to any circumstance. It suggests resilience, meaning that we have the ability to bounce back even from the most difficult times…Your ability to thrive depends, in the end, on your attitude to your life circumstances. Take everything in stride with grace, putting forth energy when it is needed, yet always staying calm inwardly. (Ping Fu)

Let the bamboo serve to remind you of all the important yet simple lessons it symbolizes. It is now up to you to put these lessons of resilience into daily use through practice and perseverance. Just remember, you don't need to be perfect…you need only to be resilient. This is the greatest lesson from the bamboo.

The Power of Superheroes

We resonate with the themes in the stories, with the dilemmas and problems that superheroes face, and we aspire to their noble impulses and heroic acts. We identify—or would like to identify—with them. Superheroes are models for us, and they are modeled after us.

—Robin S. Rosenberg, PhD

Who is your all-time-favorite superhero? Is it Batman, Superman, Wonder Woman, Supergirl, Iron Man, Spider-Man, the Hulk, Captain America, Batgirl, Thor, or Daredevil? On a personal note…My favorite is Wonder Woman. Her position is both a powerful and graceful representation of women. She exemplifies a fearless ambassador for peace. She is strong, smart, and independently liberated. She is complex but still maintains a balance of peaceful diplomacy and strategic fighting. Now think of your favorite superhero…What makes him or her a superhero? What magical powers do all superheroes possess that make them so unstoppable?

It's not just their big muscles, drop-dead-gorgeous bodies, ironclad power suits, perfect hair, or fancy capes that differentiate them as world-renowned superhero icons! It's a combination of their strength, perseverance, confidence, and passion that puts them in a league of their own and instills in them their magical powers! They are the elite players. They don't settle for mediocrity. They show up, and they show up to win the VICTORY! The battle first begins in their mind, when they consciously decide that they are claiming the VICTORY! The rest is just a self-fulfilling prophecy. Since their core fundamentals, values, emotions, thoughts, belief systems, and actions are in alignment with victory, they're able to manifest it.

In my attempts to research superheroes, I discovered something that was pretty interesting. Most superheroes, well…at least the ones with positive motives…seemed to possess the same characteristics and traits. The more I researched this, the more I found it to be true—time and time again. It was very bizarre! I literally had a "superhero" epiphany!!!! The epiphany was that I must share with you, my dear "Love Visionary," the positive, persevering, and powerful characteristics and traits that these superheroes possess. Why? Because you, my "Love Visionary," are a SUPERHERO!!!!! I've listed below the top traits that I discovered through my superhero research. Please meditate over these traits, and let them inspire and motivate you to unleash your inner Superhero!

TOP POSITIVE, PERSEVERING, AND POWERFUL SUPERHERO TRAITS

1. Extraordinary powers and abilities (strengths, gifts, and talents they were born with)

2. Courage

3. A strong moral code

4. A high tolerance for pain

5. Motivation

6. A sense of responsibility

7. Loyalty

8. A fighting spirit

9. The ability to face their fears

10. Honesty

11. Commitment

12. Definitive goals

13. A firm mission

14. Crystal-clear purpose

15. Undying passion

We love our superheroes because they refuse to give up on us. We can analyze them out of existence, kill them, ban them, mock them, and still they return, patiently reminding us of who we are and what we wish we could be.

—GRANT MORRISON

Exercise: Unleash You Inner Super Hero

Superheroes are extremely resourceful and innovate. They tackle challenges and never give up...even when they fail the first, second, or hundredth time. Their heroism is born out of their personal conviction that they're needed in the fight or in the fact that the fight is worth having. Are you ready to unleash your inner superhero? My dear "Love Visionary," you are a person of great strength, perseverance, and commitment. I'm here to tell you that there is a superhero inside of each of us! It's your job to discover how to release the powers that are already inside of you! These powers are waiting to be discovered, developed, and unleashed so that you can step into your superhero self! I've attached below the top fifteen characteristics of superheroes in "question" form to help you dig down deep to uncover your superhero powers. These questions are intense, bold, and specific. They will ignite a spark in your soul that will enable you to divulge your magical powers that lie within! You do possess supernatural powers! But…in order to unleash, utilize, and live them as all superheroes do…you must first gain the clarity, confidence, and commitment to being the superhero that you truly are! You weren't created to play small. You were created to live as a superhero who will leave behind a lasting legacy of light, leadership, and love.

Superhero Q&A

1. What Extraordinary powers and abilities (strengths, gifts, and talents) do you have?

2. How do you plan on developing them? (List goals, action steps, plan, strategy.)

3. What are you most courageous about?

4. How can you develop your courage?

5. What is your "strong moral code"?

6. How can you strengthen and develop your "strong moral code"?

7. Do you have a "high tolerance for pain"?

8. How can you work on developing a "high tolerance for pain"?

9. Where does your "motivation" come from?

10. How can you strengthen and develop your "motivation"?

11. Where does your "sense of responsibility" lie?

12. How can you strengthen and develop where your "sense of responsibility" lies?

13. What are you "loyal" about?

14. How can you strengthen and develop your "loyalty"?

15. Where does your "fighting spirit" lie?

16. How can you strengthen and develop your "fighting spirit"?

17. Where does your "ability to face your fears" lie?

18. How can you strengthen and develop your "ability to face your fears"?

19. Where does your "honesty" lie"?

20. How can you strengthen and develop your "honesty"?

21. Where does your "commitment" lie?

22. How can you strengthen and develop your "commitment"?

23. What are your definitive goals?

24. How can you strengthen and develop your "definitive goals"?

25. What is your "firm mission"?

26. How can you develop and strengthen your "firm mission"?

27. What is your "crystal-clear purpose" in life?

28. How can you develop and strengthen your "crystal-clear purpose" in life?

29. What is your "undying passion" in life?

30. How can you develop and strengthen your "undying passion" in life?

Words of Wisdom from Superheroes

I think a hero is an ordinary individual who finds strength to persevere and endure in spite of overwhelming obstacles.

—Superman

It's not dying that you need to be afraid of, it's never having lived in the first place.

—The Green Hornet

Life doesn't give us purpose. We give life purpose.

—The Flash

This. This is what I am. This is who I am. Come hell or high water if I deny it, I deny everything I've ever done. Everything I've ever fought for.

—Green Arrow

If the prospect of living in a world trying to respect the basic rights of those around you and valuing each other simply because we exist are such daunting task, impossible tasks then what sort of world are we left with? And what sort of world do you want to live in?
It's not who I am underneath, but what I do that defines me.

—Batman

Life is locomotion. IF you're not moving you're not living. But there comes a time when you've got to stop running AWAY from things and you've got to start running TOWARD something. You've got to forge ahead. Keep moving. Even if your path isn't lit trust that you'll find your way.

—THE FLASH

It doesn't matter what the newspapers say or the politicians or the whole world. They don't define who you are. You do. And not by your words, but by your actions. The truth will come out. But until then, I'm going to keep fighting, just like you do.

—CAPTAIN AMERICA

When you decide not to be afraid, you can find friends in super unexpected places.

—MS. MARVEL

No matter how bad things get, something good is out there, just over the horizon.

—THE GREEN LANTERN

You're much stronger than you think you are. Trust me.

—SUPERMAN

You only have your thoughts and dreams ahead of you. You are someone. You mean something.

—BATMAN

I have no idea where I'm going to be tomorrow. But I accept the fact that tomorrow will come. And I'm going to rise to meet it.

—Donna Troy, *Titans/Young Justice: Graduation Day*

With great power comes great responsibility.

—Uncle Ben

Dreams save us. Dreams lift us up and transform us. And on my soul, I swear until my dream of a world where dignity, honor, and justice becomes the reality we all share, I'll never stop fighting. Ever.

—Superman

Angels, Unicorns, and Miracles

I love Doreen Virtue! She is a lifelong clairvoyant who works with the angelic realm. She is author of *Healing with the Angels, How to Hear Your Angels, Messages from Your Angels,* and many more amazing books on spirituality. Doreen has appeared on *Oprah, CNN, The View,* and many other popular television and radio programs to be interviewed about her special gifts and spiritual abilities. She is a one-of-a-kind woman who leads her life with the divine purpose to give love to others. I follow her posts on Instagram; every day she shares messages of love and angel card readings. Her card readings are always "spot on" for me in that they are applicable to whatever I'm going through in my life. They always motivate, inspire, and encourage me.

Today as I was reading her message, I felt extremely called to share it with you. This message is about a "unicorn"! You're probably thinking that I've gone crazy!?!?! Well, we're all a little crazy, but open your heart and mind to the magical message that Doreen has for us. When I first discovered Doreen and her work, I will definitely admit that I thought that she was way out there! But the more I opened my heart and mind to her divine words of wisdom, passion, and power…I realized that she is undeniably a magical woman! Why is it that we have allowed ourselves to lose our childhood ability to believe in "BIG miracles and magic"? When you were a child, the world was a different place for you. You experienced life in such a drastically different way than you do know! Why? Well, when you were younger you allowed yourself to BELIEVE in the bigger, brighter, powerful, mystical, and magical elements of the world. This expanded your Universe, and as a result of believing, you experienced a reality that was more—bigger, brighter, more powerful, mystical, and magical. You were given the power to be more creative, carefree, courageous, adventurous, and fearless. Why did you ever stop believing? As you grew older…you let the opinions, thoughts, beliefs and words of others and our SSS shape your mind-set and belief system. As the years passed, it didn't take too long until you no longer believed in the Universe. I can tell you one thing… this new "adult" world that you're now living in is desperately calling you to believe in the mystical, magical, and miraculous Universe that we all live in! You need to "wake up" and believe! You're destined to live and experience the magic and miracles that our powerful Universe has in store for you. But you must be willing to believe in something far greater than your-self! For when you BELIEVE, you will RECEIVE.

The following is Doreen Virtue's Instagram post.

Yay, the Unicorn card showed up for you today! This shows that you're an indi-vidualist who's unafraid to be real and unique! You're highly creative and you're tapped-in to divinely inspired ideas. The Unicorn represents the best of you, and your highest possibility. Strive to take love-based actions which are empowered by your confidence of God working through you. You Inner Child is also ask-ing for your attention, with nurturing, and imagination, and playfulness. Wear rainbow colors, and express your "inner unicorn" This is also a sign of purifica-tion, including detoxing, and reducing negativity. It's a good idea to spend time outdoors and make changes to give yourself more freedom. Like the Unicorn, you are rare and uncommon. Allow the spirit of the Unicorn to show you how beautiful and amazing your uniqueness is!

Wasn't that a pretty incredible reading? As a young child, you probably read about mythical unicorns. You know them as the majestic white horses with a single long horn on their heads. Some stories portrayed this beautiful horn as a shiny pearl-white color, while other fantasy stories depicted it as a rainbow-colored horn. While many of the other characters in our childhood mythical storybooks were man-eating monsters or evil spirits, the unicorns stood out as the magical, peaceful, and powerful creatures. Even today, they still remain objects of wonder and beauty, as they often make appearances in popular books, television shows, and movies. They symbolize majesty, power, and strength. You, my dear "Love Visionary," are a unicorn!

The meaning of the unicorn is all about opening up to the infinite possibilities that surround you and that are available to you at all times. Many times you can't see that possibilities surround you or even that they exist. The unicorn will give you the "eyes to see" those possibilities and the wisdom to take advantage of them and to pursue your dreams. Believing in the unicorn gives you a choice to either stay living in the realms of your fears and self-imposed boundaries or to venture out of your comfort zone and ride the winds of miraculous magic! Magic and miracles are waiting for you.….All you have to do is BELIEVE and take action toward creating your dreams!

Words of Wisdom on Unicorns

A Unicorn is somebody who knows they're magical and isn't afraid to show it.

—Brittany S. Pierce from *Glee*

When someone told me I lived in a Fantasy Land, I nearly fell off my unicorn.

—AUTHOR UNKNOWN

When I look at myself in the mirror, I see a Unicorn. A bad-ass Unicorn.

—SEBASTIAN MILON

The Unicorn doesn't know how rare a thing she is and so she runs along the shore and dances in the winds and tells her clever stories and sings her pretty songs and all the others simply watch and hope to sing along.

—AUTHOR UNKNOWN

"Well, now that we have seen each other," said the Unicorn, "if you'll believe in me, I'll believe in you."

—LEWIS CARROLL

Make your life story so amazing that Unicorns have trouble believing it is true.

—KAREN SALMANSOHN

Unicorns are awesome. I am awesome. Therefore, I am a Unicorn.

—AUTHOR UNKNOWN

Happiness is believing in Unicorns.

—AUTHOR UNKNOWN

The last Unicorn is in our presence.

—OLIVIA

Where there is joy, laughter, and magic Unicorns will be found.

—AUTHOR UNKNOWN

CHAPTER 16

Creative Visualization

YOU MUST LEARN how to practice "creative visualization"! The ability to visualize yourself already in possession of—or in the physical state of—your goals, dreams, and vision is one of the most important elements of creation with "Love Vision" in order to create a life that you truly love. You must be able to visualize your goals, vision, dreams, and desires in order to gain the true passion and motivation your mind, body, and soul need in order to take action and manifest their reality.

The following is the definition of "creative visualization" from Wikipedia. It also includes discussion on the therapeutic benefits that can be gained by individuals who are suffering from physical, psychological, or emotional pain.

> **"Creative Visualization"** is the cognitive process of purposefully generating visual mental imagery, with eyes open or closed, simulating or recreating visual perception, in order to maintain, inspect, and transform those images, consequently modifying their associated emotions or feelings, with intent to experience a subsequent beneficial physiological, psychological, or social effect, such as expediting the healing of wounds to the body, minimizing physical pain, alleviating psychological pain including anxiety, sadness, and low mood, improving self-esteem or self-confidence, and enhancing the capacity to cope when interacting with others.

Visual and Nonvisual Mental Imagery

The brain is capable of creating other types of mental imagery—in addition to visual images—to simulate or recreate perceptual experience across all sensory modalities, including auditory imagery of sounds; gustatory imagery of tastes; olfactory imagery of smells; motor imagery of movements; and haptic imagery of touch, incorporating texture, temperature, and pressure.

Notwithstanding the ability to generate mental images across sensory modalities, the term "creative visualization" signifies the process by which a person specifically generates and processes visual mental imagery. All mental imagery, including the visual images generated through creative visualization, can precipitate or be associated with strong emotions or feelings.

Therapeutic Application

The therapeutic application of creative visualization aims to educate the patient in altering mental imagery, which in turn contributes to emotional change. The process facilitates the patient in replacing images that aggravate physical pain, exacerbate psychological pain, reaffirm debilitation, recollect and reconstruct distressing events, or intensify disturbing feelings such as hopelessness and anxiety. These images are replaced with imagery that emphasizes and precipitates physical comfort, cognitive clarity, and emotional equanimity.

Exercise: How to Practice and Exercise Creative Visualization

Get ready to be refreshed, renewed, and reinvigorated! Practicing "creative visualization" is super easy, so don't stress! You can practice "creative visualization" when you are alone, having a conversation with someone, or even in a large crowd of people. You can exercise it during your ride to work in the morning, in your office, while spending time with others, and even in stressful situations…like a heated argument or a disagreement.

All you need to do is clear your mind of all negativity, stress, doubt, and fear. You need to totally detox your mind of all the crap! You know what I'm talking about.. The self-doubt, negative bull sh*t, and fear that is holding you back! You need to replace that fear with LOVE, and focus your mind solely on what it is that you love, what it is that you want to create, or what you want to happen in your current situation, whatever that may be.

You must "ENVISION" your vision, desires, desired outcomes, and dreams exactly as you want them to be. You must get completely "Clear, Concise, and Creative." This is the secret key in manifesting your creative visualization in order to fulfill your true desires and live a life that you love! Please refer back to your own "Personal Vision" that you wrote in your "Love Vision" journal. Read over your personal vision several times until you can really start to visualize your desired goals and dreams.

I am a firm believer in meditation and visualization. You must give yourself the gift to meditate and visualize each and every day. This can be done virtually anywhere, and it is absolutely free! You need to be able to give yourself the mental space, time, and freedom to explore your innermost thoughts, feelings, emotions, dreams, and desires. Through meditating and creative visualization, your mind will begin to expand, and you will begin to gain insight and clarity on your goals, desires, dreams, and destiny.

You need to "energetically" align your mind, body, and spirit to fully focus and visualize every single detail of your desires. Let your mind, body, and soul visually see what this looks like, feels like, smells like, and even tastes like. You must allow your physical, emotional, psychological, and spiritual self to creatively visualize your goals and dreams exactly how you desire them to be. This "creative visualization" will elevate you energetically and will in turn produce positive emotions and feelings that will enable you to take the appropriate actions and behaviors that are necessary to manifest your VISION, desires, and dreams.

CHAPTER 17

Emotions and Feelings 101

DO YOU KNOW that your emotions and feelings have the power to create your future? They are the underlying roots in our lives. If these roots are watered, healthy, and nourished, they will allow our goals, desires, and dreams to grow, flourish, and blossom so that we can fulfill our destinies.

Dictionary.com defines the word emotion as the following: "(1) an effective state of consciousness in which joy, sorrow, fear, hate, or the like, is experienced, as distinguished from cognitive and volitional states of consciousness; and (2) any of the feelings of joy, sorrow, fear, hate, love, etc."

Merriam-Webster defines the word feeling as "an emotional state or reaction."

As humans, we experience a wide range of emotions and feelings, positive and negative. They enable us to have subjective experiences that shape our daily lives. The role of our emotions and feelings drastically influences the way in which we live. They shape the way we feel, think, learn, set and accomplish goals, and even how we perform our daily tasks. More importantly, they affect the way in which we view ourselves, others, and the world. As a result, they determine our choices and the way in which we treat ourselves and others.

It's quite simple. Positive emotions and feelings will yield positive results. Negative emotions and feelings will produce negative results. The degree to which we allow ourselves to "feel" our emotions directly leads us to mind-body experiences. The "mind-body" connection between our emotions and physiological states is very real. History and science have proven for centuries the extreme power of the mind-body connection.

You Are a Powerful Transmitter

You will attract that which is in alignment with your state of being, and you'll repel that which is out of sync with your state. If your energetic self radiates anger, frustration, and stress, this is what your physical reality will be. If your energetic self radiates love, happiness, and success, that is what your physical reality will be. The energetic signals that we are constantly sending out to the Universe are extremely complex, as their power manifests our reality. The choice is yours. You are the one who is completely responsible for the vibrations that you transmit.

You need to awaken to this super powerful law of the Universe and accept that your vibrational self (your emotions, feelings, and thoughts) attracts compatible patterns. This truth gives you an immense amount of power in manifesting your desires by allowing you to consciously change your emotions, feelings, and thoughts so that you can transmit positive vibrations into the Universe.

The Life-Changing "Channeling Method"

So, what exactly is the life-changing "channeling method"? It's one of the simplest yet most powerful methods to change your life. In entails five intimate steps that you must learn in order to get your mind, body, and soul into a state of "flow" that will allow you to channel positive emotions, feelings, and thoughts. This technique will seriously change you and your life forever! It will take you from "surviving" to "thriving" so that you can "channel" your highest self and live out your fullest potential. Outlined below you will find the five steps of the "channeling method."

Choose It, Feel It, Be It, Live It, Love It!

Step One: Choose it

Step Two: Feel it

Step Three: Be it

Step Four: Live it

Step Five: Love it

Step One: Choose It

You have the amazing power of "free will"! It is up to you each and every day to make the decision to exert this "free will" to make the conscious decision to choose the emotions, feelings, and thoughts that you want to experience on a daily basis. It is extremely important for you to realize that you are the master of your "free will" and that you must choose the emotions, feelings, and thoughts that will support you and your goals, dreams, and desires. If you don't make the conscious effort each and every day to choose that which will support you, you will remain at a very high risk for negative emotions and feelings to take control. It's simply a choice. You must "choose" the emotions, feelings, and thoughts that you want to experience and all of those that will support you and your vision.

STEP TWO: FEEL IT

You have to let your mind, body, and soul "feel it"—your desired emotions, feelings, and thoughts. You're probably thinking…how in the world you can "feel" positive emotions when you're in stressful, sad, intense, and difficult situations. The secret is that…you need to learn how to channel positive energy, so you can harness the power of your own emotions.

One of the best and easiest ways to channel this energy is through utilizing positive affirmations that use the emotions and feelings you want to experience. For example, if you are in a difficult or negative environment, situation, or emotional state….focus on "channeling" the positive emotions, feelings, and thoughts that you need to help guide you and give you the strength, peace, and courage that you need to handle the situation.

I am a big fan of using the "write-it-speak-it-feel-it" exercise. This exercise requires you to write your positive emotion or affirmation, speak it out loud at least three times, and "feel it," which requires you to meditate on your positive statement and allow your mind, body, and soul to shift and experience your desired emotions, feelings, and thoughts. For example, if you are feeling very stressed out and upset, you could use the following positive affirmation: "I am peaceful. I am peaceful. I am peaceful." If you are feeling very lonely and unloved, you could use the following affirmation: "I deeply love myself. I deeply love myself. I deeply love myself." The best part about using this special exercise is that you get to create the positive affirmations you desire to manifest…so the possibilities are endless!

STEP THREE: BE IT

Next, you must "be it"! Now that you have chosen and felt your desired emotions, feelings, and thoughts, it is imperative that you align your mind, body, and soul to be "in sync" with your desired states. By doing this, you will enter into a "state of flow" that will have a tremendous beneficial effect on your mind, body, and emotions. Your complete being and essence will become one and at peace with your emotional state.

Scientists believe that the human body contains around thirty-seven trillion cells. These cells are the "life force" of our existence. They give us the energy, strength, and vitality to live our lives. Studies have proven that through exerting positive mental and emotional states, one can literally alter their body's cellular communication process. Through this change in positive cellular communication, one's behavior can be altered as well as the body's ability to heal itself.

When negative emotions, feelings, and thoughts (noise, chaos, and misinformation) enter into one's cellular communication process, the human body suffers. Our minds, bodies, and souls provide guidance for maintaining the intercellular communication process that is essential for our cells' growth. This is why many scientists believe that the human mind's ability to operate beyond the physical realm enables humans to have an innate power to influence physical processes in their own bodies, thus leading to the healing process. This evidence strongly implies that one's emotions, feelings, and thoughts can directly change the shape and state of the molecules in the human body. As a result, this changes the vibrations in one's body.

We must make the conscious effort to "tune in" to our mind, body, and soul on a daily basis and choose to operate from an unconditional state of love. If we do this, we will be giving our body's trillions of cells the gift to "thrive" in a state of love, as opposed to just "surviving" in an environment that may be polluted with negative emotions, feelings, and thoughts that are led by fear. Choose love, and "be it"! This state of love will foster healing for your mind, body, and soul.

STEP FOUR: LIVE IT

In order to have the channeling method change your life, you must be willing to make a commitment to "live it"! You must be dedicated to daily "channeling" the positive emotions, feelings, and thoughts that will support you, your goals, and vision. You must use this method daily and "live it" until the process of "channeling" becomes like breathing to you. When you make this a part of your life, and get use to the process… positive emotions, feelings, and thoughts will become as necessary for your body as is oxygen.

You will need to "live it" through allowing your new positive emotional state and mind-set to motivate you to take the appropriate actions that are necessary to accomplish your goals. Every day you will be taking action, big steps and little steps. Some days you may feel that these steps aren't taking you in the direction of your desires. But don't give up! Perseverance will reward you greatly as you continue on your journey. All of these steps are slowly leading you to the path that you are destined to be on!

When you are "living it," you will be in a state of "flow" that will allow the Universe to supply all of your needs so that you can fulfill your dreams. Choose to "live it," and you will be able to live a lifestyle of love that will support your mind, body, and soul.

STEP FIVE: LOVE IT

Now that you are living in a state of unconditional love toward yourself, others, and the Universe, it is time for you to "love it"! Every day…you must "love it"! You must express gratitude to the Universe every day for your blessings and the life that you've been given. Regardless of your past, current circumstances, and fears…choosing and "channeling" love (positive emotions, thoughts, and feelings) will enable you to live a life of freedom. You will be able to live a life full of abundance! You will be inspired with a renewed sense of hope, faith, courage, and strength. Your passion will ignite you to fully live a life that you love!

"Loving it" and expressing gratitude is a daily choice that you must make every morning when you wake up. You must acknowledge your thanks and gratitude to the Universe every single day, no matter what. Through expressing gratitude, you will be automatically "channeling" to the highest frequency of love. The Universe will respond. This is where miracles happen.

Exercise: The "Channeling Method"

Get ready to experience the life-changing "channeling method"! This exercise should be performed daily so that it automatically becomes part of your daily life. It's quite simple. I've attached below a full list of positive emotions and feelings. Read through the list, and circle those that you want to incorporate into your life. If there are other emotions and feelings that you want to feel and experience that aren't on the list, make sure that you add them to create your own personalized list. This list can be changed on a monthly, weekly, or even daily basis. The whole purpose of this list is that it is personalized to serve you and support your highest potential.

Next, get ready to take these positive emotions and feelings and incorporate them into your life by using the five-step process of the "channeling method." Allow this process to condition your mind, body, and soul into a state of "flow" that will summon the highest frequency of energy into your life—the energy of LOVE. You must remember...that all positive emotions and feelings come from love, which is the Universe's most powerful life force.

The Five-Step Process of the "Channeling Method"

- **Step One**: Choose it

- **Step Two**: Feel it

- **Step Three**: Be it

- **Step Four**: Live it

- **Step Five**: Love it

Positive Emotions and Feelings List

Able	Absolved	Abundant	Acceptable	Accepted	Accepting	Accomplished	Accountable
Adaptable	Adequate	Admirable	Admired	Adored	Affluent	Agreeable	Alert
Appreciated	Appreciative	Approved	Approving	Assertive	Assured	At Ease	Attached
Authentic	Awake	Aware	Awesome	Balanced	Beautiful	Believing	Blessed
Brave	Bright	Brilliant	Calm	Capable	Captivated	Cared For	Carefree
Cautious	Centered	Certain	Cheerful	Cherished	Clean	Clear	Collected
Committed	Compassionate	Complete	Composed	Comprehending	Confident	Congruent	Connected
Content	Cooperative	Courageous	Credible	Daring	Decisive	Defended	Delighted
Dignified	Discerning	Disciplined	Distinguished	Dutiful	Dynamic	Eager	Easy Going
Efficient	Elated	Elegant	Elevated	Emancipated	Empowered	Encouraged	Energetic
Euphoric	Exceptional	Excited	Exhilarated	Experienced	Expressive	Exuberant	Faithful
Firm	Flexible	Flowing	Focused	Forceful	Forgiven	Fortified	Fortunate
Fulfilled	Gentle	Genuine	Gifted	Glowing	Good	Graceful	Gracious
Growing	Guarded	Happy	Harmonious	Healed	Helpful	Heroic	High
Honored	Hopeful	Humble	Humorous	Important	In Control	Included	Independent
Innocent	Inspired	Intelligent	Interested	Invigorated	Invincible	Invited	Jovial
Judicious	Kind	Learning	Liberated	Light	Lighthearted	Loose	Loved
Magnetic	Marvelous	Masterful	Mature	Meek	Merciful	Methodical	Mindful
Neat	Noble	Observant	Open	Open Hearted	Organized	Pacified	Pampered
Patient	Peaceful	Perfect	Persevering	Pleasant	Pleased	Popular	Positive
Precious	Prepared	Present	Productive	Proficient	Progressive	Prosperous	Protected
Purified	Purposeful	Qualified	Quick	Quiet	Radiant	Rational	Reasonable
Recognized	Redeemed	Regenerated	Relaxed	Reliable	Relieved	Remembered	Replenished
Respectful	Responsive	Restored	Revitalized	Rewarded	Rooted	Satisfied	Secure
Sensational	Sensible	Sensitive	Serene	Settled	Sharing	Simple	Skillful
Spirited	Splendid	Stable	Steadfast	Stengthened	Strong	Successful	Supported
Teachable	Temperate	Tenacious	Tender	Thankful	Thoughtful	Thrilled	Tolerant
Trusting	Understanding	Understood	Undisturbed	Unhurried	Unique	United	Unselfish
Valuable	Valued	Virile	Vital	Warm	Wealthy	Willing	Wise

Worthy	Yielding	Zealous	Achieving	Ambitious	Attentive	Blissful	Careful
Conscious	Dependable	Ecstatic	Energized	Fantastic	Free	Gratified	Honest
Infatuated	Joyful	Loyal	Modest	Pardoned	Powerful	Prudent	Reassured
Resolute	Selfless	Smooth	Sustained	Tranquil	Upheld	Wonderful	Active
Amused	Attractive	Bonded	Caring	Comforted	Constant	Desirable	Edified
Enthusiastic	Favored	Friendly	Grounded	Honorable	Influential	Jubilant	Lucky
Motivated	Passion	Praised	Punctual	Receptive	Respected	Self-Reliant	Soothed
Tactful	Triumphant	Valiant	Worthwhile	Blissful	Zen	High	Grateful

Developing Your Own Personal "MANTRA"

"MANTRAS" are extremely powerful! They are additional tools that you can use while meditating or practicing creative visualization to enhance or completely alter your current emotional, physical, mental, psychological, and spiritual states to those that you energetically desire.

Merriam-Webster gives a very simple definition of the word "MANTRA": "a sound, word, or phrase that is repeated by someone who is praying or meditating; a word or phrase that is repeated often or that expresses someone's basic beliefs."

Mantra's are amazing because they enable you to change your emotional state by allowing you to choose the appropriate word(s) or phrases to repeat to yourself (either verbally or silently repeated in your head) that will help energetically align your mind, body, and spirit to take the appropriate actions needed to manifest your desires.

The Power of Positive Affirmations

"Positive affirmations" are very powerful tools that you can use to unleash your full potential for love, health, wealth, success, self-esteem, peace, and happiness. Changing your thoughts can drastically change your life. We have been conditioned by our society, and we strongly hold certain belief systems and thoughts about ourselves, others, and the world that negatively impact our lives.

By using positive affirmations, you have the power to alter your negative belief systems and thought patterns by replacing them with a positive belief system and thought patterns. Doing this on a daily basis will enable you to become aware of your thoughts and will help you to begin eliminating the negative thoughts that are not serving you.

The process of using positive affirmations sends a message to your subconscious mind, letting you know that you are in control of creating your life. This allows your mind, body, and soul to be positively affected.

Exercise: Postive Affirmations

1. Write a list of twenty positive affirmations that you can read, write, and speak every day.

2. Make sure that they are positive.

3. I suggest writing your positive affirmations in the past or present tense, not the future tense. Example: "I am full of love." Remember, "LOVE" is the strongest emotion (vibrational frequency) you can send out to the Universe. By writing your affirmations as if they have already happened, or as if they are happening, you are putting your mind and body in the correct state. As a result, your energy vibrations and emotions will become positive, and your mind, body, and soul will carry out the needed actions to manifest your desires.

4. To optimize the effectiveness of your positive affirmations and to begin to see results, read your twenty positive-affirmation statements three times a day for thirty days straight. I suggest reading, writing, and speaking your affirmations aloud, as this will help your mind, body, and soul to acclimate toward their truth. Using the affirmations for a period of thirty days or longer allows for them to permeate your consciousness and become part of you.

5. I've listed some of my favorite positive affirmation statements below. You can use these as part of your twenty positive affirmations to get started. I've separated them into the following affirmation categories: Health, Mental, Emotional, Spiritual, Relationships, Career, Wealth and Prosperity, and Forgiveness. I highly suggest adding your own statements to each category, as they will encourage you to manifest your personal desires.

Positive-Affirmation Statements

HEALTH

I am extremely healthy.
I feel extremely healthy.
I am beautiful.
I feel extremely alive and invigorated!
I am strong.
I perform self-love and care daily.
I have balance in my life.

I am full of energy and life.

I am passionate about living my healthiest life!

I am passionate about nurturing my mind, body, and soul with my healthy lifestyle.

I am healed.

Every cell of my body is healed.

My body is nourished by the healthy foods that I eat.

My mind, body, and soul are healthy, connected, and in balance.

MENTAL

I am constantly in a positive "FLOW."

I love my life!

My life is easy and fun!

My mind is extremely aware and in tune to accept divine wisdom and direction from all sources of the Universe in order to be guided to fulfill my destiny.

My mind is always in a state of clarity.

I am calm.

I am extremely creative.

I am extremely brave.

I am courageous.

I am very driven.

I am always inspired.

I am constantly blessed with amazing opportunities.

I am focused and receive divine guidance from my intuition and the Universe to manifest my desires.

I am determined to fulfill my goals, dreams, and destiny.

I am the creator of my own life experiences.

Emotional

I am full of love.
I am happy.
I am grateful for my life.
I am peaceful.
I am confident.
I am joyful.
I am passionate.
I am fearless.

Spiritual

I am filled and surrounded by love.
I really love myself and nurture my mind, body, and soul.
I am full of faith.
I am full of hope.
I am at peace.
I am blessed by God's grace.
My life is in harmony.
I am a spiritual leader.
I am optimistic and am constantly blessed with amazing opportunities to help me fulfill my destiny.
The Universe totally supports me and sends me exactly what I need to fulfill my destiny.
I am mindful.

I am positive about my life and know that the Universe is sending me everything that I need to manifest my dreams.

I am a "LOVE VISIONARY."

RELATIONSHIPS

My relationships are full of love, care, and affection.

My relationships are deep and meaningful.

I have relationships built on trust, respect, and honesty.

I am blessed to have such wonderful friends and family in my life.

I am trusted and respected in all of my relationships.

My heart is open to receiving love.

I am worth loving.

I am ready for my soul mate.

My friendships and family relationships are strong, supportive, and full of love.

I have a deep sense of belonging in all of my relationships.

I am surrounded by people who are good for me and who care for me.

CAREER

I am ambitious and am focused on achieving all of my goals and dreams.

I am extremely disciplined and diligent regarding my work, career, goals, desires, and dreams.

I am brilliant at business and succeed in everything that I do.

I am extremely successful and am blessed to constantly meet and work with successful people who will help me to fulfill my dreams and destiny.

I am dependable.

I excel at everything that I focus my mind on.

I am proactive.

My life is balanced with work and play.

I am committed to taking the actions that are needed to accomplish my goals, desires, and dreams.

WEALTH AND PROSPERITY

I have an extremely abundant life.

I am wealthy.

I receive wealth, abundance, and all of the resources that I need to fulfill my destiny from the Universe.

I live in complete financial freedom.

My financial freedom allows me to live a life that I love.

My financial freedom allows me to pursue my dreams.

I prosper in all areas of my life—my mind, body, and soul are blessed.

FORGIVENESS

I forgive myself, and I am now set free.

I forgive everyone in my past who has hurt me. I release the hurt and send them love.

I release all of my hurts and resentments. I receive only love.

I forgive myself for the mistakes and bad choices that I've made. I have a beautiful life and future ahead of me. I have the power to make the changes to transform my life.

I forgive myself for letting others hurt me. I now realize that I am in control of my emotions and have the power to let no one change my emotional state of love and happiness.

Your Positive Affirmations

The Four Fundamentals—Presence, Passion, Preparation, and Perseverance

Your "presence, passion, preparation, and perseverance" are the four key fundamentals that are required in order for you to "LIVE OUT" your vision and purpose. Living in our "SSS," we have become conditioned to have our desires and dreams instantly fulfilled. All of our social outlets and the media send us the message that we should have the things that we desire instantaneously—hence how Instagram got its name.

Maybe not…but the point that I'm trying to make is that we live in a day in age in where people want things immediately. Unfortunately, this is impossible. As a result, most people in today's world are frustrated, angry, unfulfilled, and unhappy because their expectations, needs, and desires aren't getting met. What most people don't realize is that it takes time to achieve your goals, desires, and dreams. Everyone is on his or her own unique path, and each person has a different time clock in regards to their dreams.

You must be willing to remain fully present in your life so that you can be the best version of yourself, no matter the circumstances you're facing. Every day you need to remind yourself to fully live, laugh, and love…for this will allow you to live a life of joy, abundance, and peace. Since God/Higher Power/Universe has a plan for you and your life, you need to realize that you're not completely in control over the time that it will take to unfold. God/Higher Power/Universe is in control of that time clock. Most of the time, it takes us as human beings time to learn the lessons that we need in order to be granted the wisdom, guidance, and clarity that will enable us to fulfill our purpose. But don't be discouraged; every day, week, month, or year is a step. Some of these steps are bigger than others. Each step is an important lesson that is preparing you for what lies ahead. Every single step, step-by-step, is guiding you to stay course on the path that will allow you to fulfill your God-given destiny.

Even though you don't have complete control over the clock of your life, there are a lot of things that you can do that will enable you to have time work in your favor when it comes to manifesting your dreams. I've listed below the four key fundamentals that I believe will allow you to work with God/Higher Power/Universe in order to start living in a manner that will allow you to "LIVE OUT" your VISION. Step-by-step, when following these principles…you will be able to live your purpose.

1. **Presence:** Live each and every day fully present in your life. Be the best version of yourself that you possibly can be. "LIVE OUT" your VISION daily. Be fully present, and choose the actions that will manifest your dreams.

2. **Passion:** Possess a heart full of PASSION that is dedicated to living a life of perseverance and purpose. Maintain a strong FAITH in God/Higher Power/ Universe.

3. **Preparation:** Live in state of ALIGNMENT. You must align your thoughts, emotions, belief system, habits, behaviors, and actions to supportively ALIGN with your VISION, goals, desires, and dreams. As the NIKE brand tells us "JUST DO IT," you need to "JUST DO IT." All of the work and action will prepare you to fulfill your VISION. Preparation will grant you the priceless gift of blessing you with invaluable experiences, wisdom, guidance, and skills and abilities that will enable you to manifest your VISION into reality.

4. **Perseverance:** Stay 100 percent committed and dedicated to your VISION, goals, desires, and dreams. Work your A** off as you "LIVE" your VISION, and make progress toward achieving your goals, desires, and dreams.

Living and applying these principles on a daily basis is a nonnegotiable for you, my dear "Love Visionary"! They are necessary in order for you to take immediate action and start "LIVING" your VISION now. Fear and distraction are your two worst enemies when it comes to manifesting your dreams. In following either, you will be deterred from your destined path and led on a hopeless, unfulfilling, and purposeless journey.

Although, we unfortunately at times let fear and distractions captivate us. They steal our attention, emotional energy, and efforts, deterring us from our destined paths. This is why it is so necessary for you to live in a state of full awareness so that you can catch yourself when you fall victim to your fears and the distractions of life. Once you recognize that you have fallen victim, it is your responsibility to redirect your mind, body, and soul back to following the path of love. In doing so, you will continue on your destined path. Step-by-step, you will be divinely guided with passion and purpose. You, my beautiful "Love Visionary," are called to do great and mighty things in this life! For God/Higher Power/The Universe has plans for you and your life that are beyond your wildest dreams!

Words of Wisdom from Scripture

"For I know the plans I have for you," declares the Lord, "plans to prosper you and not to harm you, plans to give you hope and a future."

—Jeremiah 29:11 NIV

My Personal Experience with the Four Fundamentals

The four fundamentals are present in everyone's life. Whether you realize it or not, your presence, passion, preparation, and perseverance have greatly shaped the course of your life. They have directly affected your decisions and choices in regards to the VISION that you have for your life. As a result, they have somehow directed you to where you are today. You have created your present reality from your past choices. This can be extremely hard to digest for most people since we don't like to think of the mistakes and poor choices that we've made over the years. But you need to remember that you are human. Your past doesn't define you! You have complete control and free will!

I'll be completely honest with you. Following the four fundamentals in your daily life is not easy. It requires self-sacrifice, hard work, and perseverance. Although it isn't easy... it is worth it! You are worth it! You deserve to live a life that you absolutely love! You as a "Love Visionary" are called to live your VISION, PASSION, and PURPOSE.

Disregard the persuasive messages from our "SSS" that are leaving you unfulfilled, depressed, and unhappy. It's selling you the "WANT IT/HAVE IT" principle, which is the message to you that if you want something...that you can have it instantaneously. Now that you are fully aware of those deceiving messages and lies, you can stand firm in the truth of the four key fundamentals. You now are fully aware...that in real life it takes far more than wanting something in order to "HAVE IT." What does it take? It takes YOU... your presence, passion, preparation, and perseverance to manifest your VISION. Step-by-step, when following these key fundamentals, you will be living out your "VISION." What I learned from my personal experience with living according to the four key fundamentals is that it truly takes time, hard work, passion, and perseverance to begin manifesting your dreams. Don't get discouraged! For it is the unseen God/Universe/ Higher Power that has your back and is aligning your life accordingly to orchestrate all the details that are needed to manifest your VISION.

Even after I made the life-changing decision to become a life coach and motivational speaker, it didn't happen overnight. It actually took me years of working on building my business, writing my book, coaching curriculum, hosting various women's motivational events, networking, learning social media, etc...before I even felt like I was living my dream. Why? Well, my answer is pretty simple and not too exciting.... Like everybody in the world, I had bills to pay. Lots of bills to pay. This was my reality, so in the meantime of working my A** off to build, create, and live my dream, I had to work in corporate America. This wasn't something that I was crazy about...at all! Most of you totally get this, as you probably aren't happy or fulfilled in your current job, especially if you have a specific PASSION in life. For those PASSIONISTAS (both men and women…this is just my groovy term for a person living a life that is fueled by their passion) out there who have a very clear VISION and purpose for what that they desire to "LIVE OUT"—don't be discouraged! I'm here to tell you that God/The Universe/Higher Power is using all of your hard work and perseverance to prepare you for your future. There are certain lessons that you need to learn in order to receive the wisdom and guidance from above. The work that you are currently doing and all of the work that you have done in your past is preparing and refining you. Through the various jobs that you've worked, the career that you've built, the relationships that you have developed, the family you have raised, and your self-sacrifice…..all of it together has given you the invaluable gift of special skills and abilities that will enable you to fulfill your destiny. Step-by-step, day-by-day, week-by-week, month-by-month, year-by-year…You are going through the "PREPARATION" that is needed in order to live your purpose and passion.

Sometimes as we go through this preparation, it is very hard to persevere because we become exhausted, depressed, and unfulfilled. We begin to feel as though we will never see the light at the end of the tunnel! Our hard work, dedication, and perseverance feel as though they are getting us nowhere. But we need to "WAKE UP" and acknowledge that we are the light! As a "Love Visionary" it is our responsibility to live a life of passion and purpose every day, regardless of our current circumstances. We must daily ignite the light of passion that remains inside of us so that we can move forward in the direction of our dreams. It's so easy to get caught up in the daily "grind of life"! For our to-do list of responsibilities never seems to end…from our jobs, bills, errands, family, relationships, etc…we are on a constant hamster wheel of getting stuff done. It is seriously time for you to jump off that hamster wheel of stress and to shift your perspective. You need to consciously choose an attitude of gratitude every day. When you begin each day with a grateful heart, you will be able to experience the "greatness of life" over the "grind of life." Through shifting your mind, body, and soul to a state of gratitude, you will be able to live the four key principles effortlessly as God/The

Universe/Higher Power takes you to places that you never even dreamed were possible! You will be guided every step of the way. Maintain your passion and perseverance, for they will not lead you astray.

Exercise:
Defining Your Presence, Passion, Preparation, and Perseverance

I truly believe that writing is cathartic. It allows you to deeply express your most personal experiences and deepest emotions. It creates a safe space (nonjudgment zone) where you can freely unleash whatever it is that you desire. As a result, this allows you to gain clarity, courage, confidence and, most importantly, healing. I've designed this exercise to allow you to dig deep and to reflect on all of the life experiences and challenges that you've had, and the choices that you've made. I will ask you to expound on certain areas of your life that all relate to the four key fundamentals. The goal of this exercise is to see how far that you've come in your life, the lessons that you learned, and the progress that you've made. I want it to encourage you to know that your life has deep meaning, significance, and purpose. Allow this exercise to inspire you to continue to persevere on your never-ending journey of manifesting your dreams.

1. **Presence**: Expound on how being present in your daily life has had an effect on your life. Do you live fully present in your life? Or do you live your life disengaged, just going through the motions? Are you only experiencing the "GRIND OF LIFE," or are you experiencing the "GREATNESS OF LIFE" with a grateful heart? Feel free to write out your deepest feelings and emotions, and answer these questions openly and honestly.

2. **Passion**: Do you live a passionate life? Or do you live a passionless life? What are your true passions? What is it that you love? What passions have you pursued in your past? What passions are you currently pursing? What passions do you plan on pursuing in the future? What passions give your life purpose?

3. **Preparation**: What experiences—the jobs you've worked, your career, your relationships, your financial life, your success, your spiritual life, your health and wellness, your self-sacrifice—have prepared you? What invaluable lessons have you learned from this preparation? What gifts, talents, skills, and abilities have they given you? What guidance and wisdom have you gained from living all of these various experiences?

4. **Perseverance**: What life experiences, situations, circumstances, and challenges have you persevered through? Be specific…How have you persevered in your career, relationships, health, or wellness? What about mentally, emotionally, financially, or spiritually? Detail how you persevered, what kept you going, and the outcome that resulted. Where has your perseverance taken you? What life lessons, guidance, and wisdom did you receive from not giving up? What opportunities, connections, and life experiences were you given from your persevering spirit, passion, and hard work? How has your perseverance affected your life decisions and choices? How has your perseverance shaped your life? Be free and fearless in answering these questions, for your answers will give you more clarity on your past and even more courage to live your life to the fullest.

CHAPTER 18

Miracles and Manifestation

NOW THAT YOU have your "Love Vision" on and are ready to start living a life that you absolutely love, you must start taking immediate action on your new "Love Vision" mind-set, positive thoughts, beliefs, desires, and goals by acting "AS IF" you already are living the life of your dreams.

You need to read the following questions, and act accordingly on a daily basis as to how you answer each one. If I were living my dream life right now, how would I be living my life each day? How would I act? How would I think? What would I believe? Who would I be friends with? How would I treat people? How would I dress? What kind of self-confidence, faith, and hope would I have? Would I live out a healthier lifestyle with my diet and exercise? Would I spend more time with my friends and family each day? How would I spend my free time? How dedicated and committed would I be to my professional and personal life? How passionately and fearlessly would I live my life?

Acting "AS IF" you're currently living the life of your dreams will allow your actions, behaviors, mind-set, thoughts, emotions, belief system, and faith to align with the strongest and highest energy force (frequency) of LOVE on this planet. This intense and miraculous power of love will produce massive miracles in your life. It will allow you to "co-create" with the Universe in order to manifest your deepest desires, goals, and dreams so that you can fulfill your destiny.

Ask for Help

I'm here to tell you that you need to ask for help! You need to ask the Universe/God/Higher Power to help you fulfill your purpose. You also need to ask people—your friends, family, partner, coworkers, colleagues, business contacts, and even people you don't know that well—to help you. Why? You can't fulfill your purpose and live your VISION all by yourself. People were created together on this earth in order to love and support one another. I'm sharing this with you because it took me a long time to realize this truth. I went through a period in my life after my surgery complication that involved me trying to do a lot of things on my own. This got me nowhere. It wasn't until I surrendered to God/Universe/Higher Power that miracles started happening in my life. I've learned that if you are willing to ask for help, you will receive it.

The Universe is full of all of the resources that you need—the people, places, things, ideas, opportunities, and so on…You can't be afraid to ask for exactly what it is that you want and need. Just as the acclaimed spiritual book *The Secret* teaches—you must ASK, BELIEVE, and RECEIVE. It is in your willingness and confidence of ASKING and BELIEVING that you will be granted the ability to RECEIVE. As long as what you're asking for is in alignment with your purpose, you will be given exactly what it is that you need. Sometimes you will be given specifically what you asked for from the metaphysical world. Other times, you will receive what you need from another realm. It's in this dimension that you will receive insight and wisdom to help you physically, emotionally, mentally, and spiritually. Not all of what you think you need is in the realms of this physical world. Most of what we truly need is the gift of divine guidance. So I deeply encourage you to ASK and BELIEVE, for you will receive miracles in your life. These miracles will come to you in many different forms. Stay fully present, and be open and willing to receive.

Words of Wisdom on Miracles

Miracles occur naturally as expressions of love. The real miracle is the love that inspires them. In this sense, everything that comes from love is a miracle.

—Marriane Williamson, *A Return To Love: Reflections on The Principles of A Course in Miracles*

Love List

It's time to create your "LOVE LIST"! You probably have no clue what I'm talking about…right? That's OK. Your "LOVE LIST" is your go-to resource list that you will create in order to help you live a life that you love.

Think about it…Why do you make a list of all of the foods that you need to get when you to the grocery store? The answer is simple…You don't want to forget to buy the foods that your body needs for optimal health and wellness.

So, if we utilize grocery lists and daily to-do lists to accomplish our goals….doesn't it make sense that we should have our own personal "LOVE LIST" to ensure that our personal needs and desires get fulfilled?

Exercise: Creating Your "Love List"

The purpose of building a "Love List" is to help you begin incorporating the things that you love into your daily life. Utilizing this list will help you to maintain a healthy balance and will help you to combat the stresses of life.

You can refer back to your "VISION" statement or your answers from the "YOLO" exercise to help guide you to write down all of the people, places, things, and activities that you love. Utilizing your "Love List" will enable you to nourish your mind, body, and soul so that you can live a life that you truly love and enjoy!

You *must* incorporate at least three of your "Love List" items into your life each day. The goal is to continually build your "Love List" and to start incorporating more of what you love into your daily life. I've attached below a portion of my "Love List" for you to get an idea on how to get started. Good luck.

MY LOVE LIST

- Spending time with my family

- Spending time with my friends

- Reading and being inspired by the authentic truth of others

- Writing

- Enjoying art

- Music

- Exercising

- Meditating

- Visualizing

- Going to the beach

- Positive affirmations

- Engaging in deep and meaningful conversations with others

- Building new relationships

- Strengthening current relationships that I am already blessed with

- Sunrises

- Sunsets

- Dancing

- Motivational speaking

- Sleeping in late—when I can

- Praying

- Eating healthy and nourishing my body

- Practicing acts of self-love

- Traveling

- Following my heart

- Following my intuition

- Animals

- Working as a certified life coach and helping people live lives that they love

- Creating and implementing new ideas

- Living boldly

- Living fearlessly

- Living courageously

- Living passionately

- Living a life I love

Your "LOVE LIST" will help you achieve balance in your life by allowing you to connect to your mind, body, and soul through doing the things that you "LOVE" each and every day.

Your Personal Love List

The Magical Equation for Living Your Dreams

LOVE + ACTION = LOVE-FESTATION

Love-festation is the new manifestation equation for our generation! We now hold the secret formula that will allow us to yield the results that we desire in our lives! You may be thinking…what in the world is a "Love-festation"?!?! Well, it's actually quite simple. "Love-festation" is the manifestation of your dreams through the exertion of your love and intended action.

Let "Love Vision" be your guide as you dedicate your mind, body, and soul to following your passion and taking action on your dreams. If you want to accomplish something that you LOVE, go do it! No matter what, if you take action, you will eventually end up in the right place. When you combine action with the guidance that comes from following your heart, your progress will be fast, powerful, and fulfilling.

Most people are sitting on the sidelines waiting for the "perfect moment," but unfortunately…that moment may never come. Why? Because you will be the one who is out there creating many "perfect moments"—learning, growing, doing, and succeeding. This is what will enable you to live the life of your dreams.

This powerful equation that you have just discovered has actually been around since the beginning of mankind. It is has been known and applied by some of the most creative, talented, inventive, and genius people for centuries. Think about it…Who do you know who is using this equation to manifest dreams and live a life that he or she loves?

I'll tell you who comes to my mind, from this generation….The famous and well-known inventors, scientists, artists, philosophers, humanitarians, movie producers, activists, political leaders, spiritual teachers, musicians, and actors…just to name a few. These are the individuals who are applying this magical equation to manifest their dreams.

They are out there in the world doing what they love, constantly creating exactly what it is that they desire by taking action on their passion. They're perfecting their crafts, skill sets, knowledge, and creative abilities by allowing love and action to rule their lives. They are more than dreamers and doers; they are "Love Visionaries." Are you?

Unleashing Your Inner Child

It's time to unleash your "inner child," baby! Why? I know you think I'm crazy…but right now I want you to let your mind revert back to the time when you were a child. I want you to allow your memory to take you as far back as you can remember. Focus on the memories that begin to surface. Try to focus on positive memories in which you were having fun, using your imagination, and acting out on your desires and dreams. Keep focusing on these memories and begin to meditate on what is surfacing. Let your mind and emotions stay present with these memories until things become clearer for you.

Were these memories, scenarios, images, emotions, and feelings that you experienced as a child quite different from those that you currently experience in your life? I'm sure you answered a big "YES" to that question. The reason is…that children, unless living in a negative and harmful environment, live in a state of freedom, not fear. Children have "big, beautiful, and boundary-free dreams" that allow them to live in a state of creativity, courage, and creation. Their attitudes, mind-sets, and beliefs all support their desires…as they are willing to do whatever it takes to make them happy.

They live in a state of focusing on what they want and truly desire. They will go to extreme lengths to get whatever it is that they want, even if that means taking risks. They have a sense of adventure that allows them to play out their fantasies, desires, and dreams in their everyday life. They include their friends, family, peers and even strangers to engage in their world of constant creativity. They are not embarrassed or ashamed of expressing their desires and dreams to others. Simply put…children follow their heart and invite others and the Universe to support their desires.

Why do we leave these ways of living a life we love behind as we grow older? Unfortunately, as we age….life changes us. Unless we make a conscious effort to nurture, love, and unleash our inner child on a daily basis..our inner child can die. We let life, difficult times, and hardships begin to age our souls. Fear begins to have more dominance in our lives than freedom. Our attitudes, mind-sets, and beliefs are altered. Fear encourages us to play and live safe without taking unnecessary risks and adventure. Our creative genius enters into a state of dormancy. Our lives, desires, and dreams become stagnant because our inner child is not alive.

Now is your "wake-up" call! It's time to awaken your inner child so that you can unlock your creative genius, passion, and sense of adventure to create a life that you love! Keep in mind, I'm not saying that you should revert to the behavior of a child, neglect your adult responsibilities, and just start living a lifestyle of 365 days of fun! What I am saying is that you shouldn't let your innate passion, creativity, courage, and adventure die. You need to nurture your "inner child" and refine it to fit your adult lifestyle and responsibilities. We must adapt our "inner child" to where we are at currently in our lives so that we can truly flourish, thrive, and be alive! As we begin the process of awakening, nurturing, and loving our "inner child," things will quickly begin to shift. You will go from living in a state of "surviving" to a state of "thriving"! This is where creation begins.

Exercise: Unleashing Your "Inner Child"

A Daily Exercise to Allow You to Live in a State of Freedom, Creativity, and Creation

The following questions (some of which you may have already answered in this book) are designed to help you unleash your "inner child." Record your answers to the below questions and then utilize those answers to help you write a daily "inner-child" to-do list that will be complete of activities that unleash your "inner child."

1. What unleashes your "inner child"?

2. What unleashes your creative genius?

3. What makes your heart sing?

4. What makes you smile?

5. What makes you happy?

6. What are you passionate about?

7. What motivates you?

8. What inspires you?

9. What ignites you?

10. What do you love?

11. What makes you feel loved?

12. What makes you want to love?

13. What makes you unstoppable?

14. What allows you to create?

15. What allows you to live your dream life?

16. What allows you to take action on your goals, desires, and dreams?

Your Daily "Inner-Child" To-Do: List

After recording your answers to the above questions, use the following space in your "Love Vision" journal to compile a daily "to-do list" of activities that will allow you to unleash your "inner child." I've listed a few examples of the activities that are on my personal list. Now it's time for you to build your list! Your list can include any activities that you desire.

My Daily "Inner-Child" To-Do: List

1. Write

2. Meditate

3. Dedicate time during the day for creative visualization

4. Positive affirmations

5. Connecting with friends, family, coworkers, and clients

6. Living passionately

7. Living boldly

8. Living fearlessly

9. Laughing freely

10. Loving deeply

11. Living out loud

12. Speaking my truth

13. Living authentically

14. Reading things that "awaken, motivate, and inspire" me

15. Building my faith through hope

16. Sharing with others my goals, desires, and dreams

17. Journaling

18. Praying

19. Spending time practicing the "Channeling Method"

20. Yoga

21. Fantasizing

22. Dancing

23. Painting

24. Singing in the shower

25. Cooking

26. Reading

27. Spending time in nature

28. Spending time with animals

29. Napping

30. Daydreaming

31. Taking adventurous risks

32. Asking for what I want

33. Believing in my dreams

34. Taking action to accomplish my goals, desires, and dreams

35. Communicating and creating with the Universe to manifest my goals, innermost desires, and dreams

36. Living in a state of Love

Your Daily "Inner-Child" To-Do List

Words of Wisdom from Love Visionaries

IT'S TIME TO GET INSPIRED

The path to success is to take massive, determined action.

—TONY ROBBINS

You don't learn to walk by following rules—You learn by doing, and by falling over.

—RICHARD BRANSON

Pleasure in the job puts perfection in the work.

—ARISTOTLE

You miss 100% of the shots you never take.

—WAYNE GRETZKY

Nobody knows what you can do, but you. Nobody can tell you. If I tell you all the people who told me I wasn't going to act, or sing or dance, or I wasn't good at it. Or I should stop, or I should quit, or even after I became famous, for doing things. I would be locked in a house somewhere doing nothing. The truth is, nobody knows what's inside of you. Only you know what's inside of you. Only you know what you can accomplish, and what you're capable of, and what your gut, and your dreams, and your desires and your wants and your ability. You only know, nobody else knows. So whatever you feel in your heart and in your gut, you should follow that.

—Jennifer Lopez

A leader is one who knows the way, goes the way, and shows the way.

—John C. Maxwell

Once you figure out who you are and what you love about yourself, I think it all kind of falls into place.

—Jennifer Aniston

Nothing will work unless you do.

—Maya Angelou

May the force be with you, is charming, but it's not important. What's important is that you become the Force—for yourself and perhaps for other people.

—Harrison Ford

If you believe in something great, I believe that you can achieve something great.

—Katy Perry

You can't just sit there and wait for people to give you that golden dream. You've got to get out there and make it happen for yourself.

—Diana Ross

All our dreams can come true, if we have the courage to pursue them.

—WALT DISNEY

So many of our dreams at first seem impossible, then they seem improbable, and then, when we summon on the will, they soon become inevitable.

—CHRISTOPHER REEVE

You work is to discover your work and then with all your heart to give yourself to it.

—BUDDHA

CHAPTER 19

The Power of Gratitude

DID YOU KNOW that practicing gratitude has been scientifically proven to improve one's mental, physical, emotional, and psychological health? The results of a study indicated that daily gratitude exercises resulted in higher report levels of alertness, enthusiasm, determination, optimism, and overall energy. Additionally, the gratitude group experienced less depression and stress. They also exercised more regularly and made progress toward their personal goals. The study also revealed that people who feel grateful are more likely to feel loved.

Gratitude can become a positive habit—but only with discipline. With continued exercise, practicing gratitude will create more abundance, prosperity, well-being, and happiness than you ever thought possible.

For years, Oprah Winfrey has been known for being an advocate on the power and pleasure of being grateful. She advises that if you don't feel that you have anything to be grateful for, you should start by just being grateful for your breath. She says to focus on the good that you have, not the lack of it, because whatever gets your attention will increase the energy of gratitude. That's how joy rises.

Words of Wisdom on Gratitude

This single greatest thing you can do to change your life today would be to start being grateful for what you have right now. And the more grateful you are, the more you get. The more you praise and celebrate life, the more there is in life to celebrate.

—OPRAH WINFREY

Gratitude opens the door to…the power, wisdom, the creativity of the universe. You open the door through gratitude.

—DEEPAK CHOPRA

If you're gonna make a change, you're gonna have to operate from a new belief that says life happens not to me but for me.

—TONY ROBBINS

The miracle of gratitude is that it shifts your perception to such an extent that it changes the world you see.

—DR. ROBERT HOLDEN

Gratitude unlocks the fullness of life. It turns what we have into enough, and more. It turns denial into acceptance, chaos into order, confusion to clarity.

—MELODY BEATTIE

When you practice gratitude, there is a sense of respect towards others.

—THE DALAI LAMA

Showing gratitude is one of the simplest yet most powerful things humans can do for each other.

—RANDY PAUSCH

No gesture is too small when done with gratitude.

—OPRAH WINFREY

Gratitude is the single most important ingredient to living a successful and fulfilled life.

—JACK CANFIELD

Each morning, when you open your eyes, think only three things: Thank you, thank you, and thank you. Then, set out to make the best use of the gift of this day that you can.

—WAYNE DYER

Your Gratitude will determine your altitude!!! Gratitude is like a seed that when planted and watered daily…will grow a beautiful garden of blessings in your life that will continue to grow and flourish into the lives of others. The practice of gratitude magically yields abundance to flow forth in your mind, body, and soul.

Exercise: Gratitude Journaling: 101

Develop the ritual of writing down five things that you're grateful for in your life every day. You can write your daily gratitude journal entries at any time during your day. A lot of people prefer to start their day off on a positive path by listing their gratitude items in the morning when they wake up. Others prefer to do it in the evening before they go to bed, in order to reflect and meditate on the blessings of their day. Regardless, I highly suggest you write in your gratitude journal around the same time every day, as this will allow you to develop the habit of faithfully maintaining your journal on a daily basis.

You can write your gratitude statements in a variety of ways. The most important thing is that you write your gratitude statement from your heart. You can start off by saying something like the following:

"I am grateful for _____."

"I am thankful for _____."

"Thank you, God/Higher Power/Source/Universe, for _____."

There are no specific requirements as to how you should write your gratitude statements. You can write about the little things in your day that made you smile, the person who made you feel loved, or someone who made you laugh—you choose to reflect on whatever it is no matter how big or small.

Discipline is key in making gratitude journaling a positive habit in your daily life. With continued exercise, practicing gratitude will create more abundance, prosperity, well-being, happiness, and love in your life…more than you ever imagined were possible!

MY GRATITUDE JOURNAL

Below is an excerpt from some of my personal Gratitude Journal entries over the past year.

Thank you, God, for my friends and family, who show me unconditional love and support.

Thank you, God, for my healthy body.

Thank you, God, for my creative mind.

Thank you, God, for restoring my physical vision.

Thank you, God, for allowing me to live a life full of passion and purpose.

Thank you, God, for giving me a VISION for my life that will allow me to fulfill my destiny.

Thank you, God, for providing for all of my needs at the precise time needed.

Thank you, God, for preparing my soul mate.

Thank you, God, for your strength.

Thank you, God, for your peace.

Thank you, God, for your hope.

Thank you, God, for healing my mind, body, and soul.

Thank you, God, for allowing me to show love to others.

Thank you, God, for allowing me to live a life full of faith.

Thank you, God, for allowing me to live a life full of passion and purpose.

Thank you, God, for letting me release fear.

Thank you, God, for healing my pain.

Thank you, God, for healing my heart.

Thank you, God, for taking care of me.

Thank you, God, for your forgiveness.

Thank you, God, for your grace.

Thank you, God, for your love.

Your Gratitude Journal

The Prayer for a New Day

Dear God, Thank you for this new day, its beauty and its light. Thank you for my chance to begin again. Free me from the limitations of yesterday. Today may I be reborn. May I become more fully a reflection of your radiance. Give me strength and compassion and courage and wisdom. Show me the light in myself and others. May I recognize the good that is available everywhere. May I be, this day, an instrument of love and healing, lead me into gentle pastures. Give me deep peace that I might serve you most deeply. Amen.

—Marianne Williamson, *Illuminata: Thoughts, Prayers, Rites of Passage*

CHAPTER 20

The Power of Following Your Heart

THE MIND IS absolutely amazing. It's capable of creating the most beautiful works of art, developing brilliant ideas, scientific theories, and even devising inventive solutions for complicated problems. Although there is a BIG PROBLEM!!! The mind is caught up within the physical boundaries of this world, and it has a tendency to allow fear, negative thoughts, emotions, drama, and hopelessness to penetrate our conscious and subconscious minds.

As a result, your mind can become completely out of touch with your true essence—your soul. It is your soul that contains the source of your ultimate wisdom, for it possesses the deep knowledge of who you truly are.

Whenever you're making a decision, your mind is wired to come up with a reasonable conclusion. This is why it is so tempting to listen to your rational mind, as we're expected to make rational and reasonable decisions. Disregarding your rational mind as the primary source to help you make decisions is usually frowned upon.

But when you become "in tune" to your heart and begin listening to the authentic truth that resides within your soul, miracles begin to happen. You will be guided to take the appropriate actions that are necessary to help guide you on your journey. You will begin to receive unexpected and supportive synchronicities, amazing opportunities all designed to help you manifest your deepest desires and dreams.

The Purpose of Following Your Heart

The well-known idioms "follow your heart" and "listen to your heart" have been preached for decades by some of the world's greatest spiritual teachers and successful leaders. But what does it really mean to follow your heart?

Merriam-Webster defines the "heart" in the medical sense as the following: "the organ in your chest that pumps blood through your veins and arteries." This online dictionary also describes the heart as "the place where emotions are felt; one's innermost character, feelings, or inclinations. The central or most vital part of something." The truth is…that the heart is more than just an organ in your chest. Your heart is the center of your cardio-vascular system. It is vitally responsible for just about everything that gives your body life. It's one of the most important organs and is responsible for pumping blood throughout your body and carrying all of the vital materials that your body needs in order to survive.

Ancient philosophers and scientist such as Aristotle and the Roman physician Galan deemed the heart as the seat of thought, emotion, passion, and reason. No matter how we prefer to define the heart, it is so much more that we will ever be able to describe. Why? I'll tell you exactly why…Your heart is your soul, intuition, gut feeling…It is the essence of your spiritual and emotional well-being.

Your heart is your most valuable guide and resource that lies deep within you to provide you the wisdom and direction that you need to embark on the journey that will allow you to live your life with passion and purpose. Choose to listen and follow your heart; it will not mislead you. It will allow you to fulfill your destiny.

Exercise: Heart Q & A

It's time to quiet your mind and listen to your heart. The below questions are intended to help you gain extreme clarity on your life's purpose and passions. Some of the questions were already asked in the YOLO exercise, but I want to ask you again…because they're the most important questions that you will ever be asked in your life. This time around, when you answer these questions, be as detailed as possible. The clearer you can define your passion and purpose the faster you will be able to "LIVE IT"! Be open, real, and honest…this is your life, and you were meant to live a life that you absolutely love.

- What do you love to do?

- What do you feel you were born to do?

- What are you passionate about?

- What excites you?

- What motivates you?

- What makes you happy?

- What do you feel your true calling on this earth is?

- What do you want to do with your life?

- What do you want to create in this life?

- How do you want to help others in this life?

- What truly fulfills you?

- What legacy do you want to leave behind after you leave this earth?

Exercise: Feel the Heat of Your Passion

This meditation exercise is guaranteed to refresh, rebalance, and reenergize you when you need it the most. It's designed to help you unwind, relax, and restore when you're feeling stressed out, stuck, or just plain scared of whatever situation or circumstance that you're dealing with. It will allow you to clear out all seven of your chakras. The chakras are the energy centers in your body that help your body regulate all of its processes. This includes regulating and balancing your organ function, immune system, and even your emotions. These seven chakras are the centers in your body in which your energy (life force) flows. It is believed that blocked energy in one of your chakras can lead to sickness. It is extremely important that you keep this energy freely flowing so that you can live freely, fearlessly, and full of life.

This exercise is one of my all-time favorites….because you can literally do it anywhere and at any time that you need inspiration and rejuvenation! You can perform it sitting in a chair, sitting on the floor with your legs crossed, or lying down on your back. I highly recommend (if possible), that you do this exercise lying down so that your whole body can fully relax and reap the benefits of this mind-body-soul exercise.

First, choose which position you will use. You may even be in your office at work or at home with your family or partner. It's best to have a little privacy, especially if you want to fully relax and unplug. Next, you need to close your eyes and completely "LET GO" of all of your negative thoughts, emotions, beliefs, and stress. Let it all go—totally clear your mind. Give yourself as much time as you need to completely empty out your mind. Imagine a light misting rain on your entire body, washing away all of your fears and stress. Let the beautiful crystal water wash away all of the negativity, drop by drop. Keep allowing this magical mist to clear away all toxicity from your mind, body, and soul. Continue to meditate as the rain clears your body. Take as much time that you need to meditate in this refreshing mist of healing. After you feel completely cleared of all of your fears, stress, and negativity, you will be ready to fill your body with passion, love, and positivity.

Get ready to clear and balance your chakras! Now...that you feel relaxed, take a deep breath in through your nose, and then exhale through your mouth. Continue breathing in through your nose and exhaling through your mouth. Keep this breathing technique up throughout the exercise. With every breath, release anything that you need to. Become aware of the ground or air beneath your feet (depending on how you're doing this exercise). Feel the solidness that is there.

Allow yourself to immerse your mind, body, and soul on your VISION, goals, desires, and dreams. Start to visualize and meditate on all of this....until you can literally "FEEL" your passion and desires. Visualize yourself living out your passions, purpose, goals, desires, and dreams so vividly that you can "FEEL" it. Don't restrict yourself. Let your mind, body, and soul go to wherever it feels led...You will begin to experience a "SHIFT" as your thoughts, emotions, and beliefs "SHIFT" to align with your desires. Keep meditating on your VISION and dreams. Next, let the "heat of your passion" transform into a liquid-heat "RED PASSION ENERGY." Visualize this passion-filled red-hot energy at the bottom of your feet as it begins to burn brighter and brighter. Allow it to continue to get brighter and warmer as it begins to fill the soles of your feet. You soon will feel a tingling, warm sensation in your feet. Let this continue to travel up through your calves and legs. Feel the purity and passion of this red-hot passion energy as it continues to travel up through your body.

Now the heated energy is entering your "ROOT CHAKRA." This is the chakra this is closest to the earth and is responsible for grounding you to the earth and making sure that you feel safe for your physical survival. Allow your entire root chakra (area located around your hips) to be filled with this energy. This will enable you to feel safe, secure, and more grounded with the earth. Let it continue to flow up to your "SACRAL CHAKRA." This is your chakra of desire, creativity, sexuality, and procreation. Allow the red-hot passion energy to fill up your sacral chakra; let it clear out all impurities. Let it honor and light up your creative abilities.

As the light travels up to your "SOLAR PLEXUS CHAKRA" (middle of your stomach), allow it to honor your life force. This chakra is the home of your emotional and creative life that allows you to take action and achieve your desires. Allow it to be immersed in the red-hot passion energy.....as it continues to flow up to your "HEART CHAKRA" (the space in the middle of your chest). Your heart chakra is your center of love, compassion, harmony, and peace. Release all negative emotions, fears, hurts, and insecurities. Allow the red-hot energy passion to fill your heart and ignite your deepest desires, loves, and passions.

Continue deeply inhaling through your nose and exhaling through your mouth. Inhale this red-hot energy until it travels up to your "THROAT CHAKRA." This is the chakra of communication, self-expression, and judgment. Allow your throat to loosen until you can "FEEL" your "AUTHENTIC TRUTH" ready and willing to speak. As the light clears your throat chakra, your ability to speak your "AUTHENTIC TRUTH" will be restored so that you can clearly communicate your truth, thoughts, emotions, and desires.

As the truth is opening up for you....allow the red-energy light of your passion continue to flow upward as it reaches your "THIRD-EYE CHAKRA." Allow your third-eye to be opened so that you can live fully aware of your truth, the truth in others, and the truth in the Universe around you. Opening your third eye will allow you to remain fully present and aware in your life so that you can remain fully present in living.

Take a deep breath in as the red-passion energy travels up through your "CROWN CHAKRA." This chakra is your center of connection to God and the Universe. Allow this red-hot energy to completely fill your crown chakra and connect your mind, body, and soul to your VISION, goals, desires, and dreams until you can literally feel the "HEAT" of your passion throughout your entire body. Allow this warm, tingling sensation to restore, rebalance, reenergize and heal you. Let it ignite your passion so that you are more focused, motivated, inspired, energetic, courageous, and fearless! Let the red-hot energy PASSION…continue to burn fervently in your life! Use this exercise on a daily basis so that you can live a life full of "RED-HOT STEAMING PASSION"!

Let Your Heart Be Inspired

INSPIRATIONAL WORDS BY "LOVE VISIONARIES"

Passion is the genesis of genius.

—ANTHONY ROBBINS

The most powerful weapon on earth is the human soul on fire.

—FERDINAND FOCH

Let yourself be silently drawn by the strange pull of what you really love. It will not lead you astray.

—JALALUDDIN RUMI

Your time is limited, so don't waste it living someone else's life. Don't be trapped by dogma, which is living with the results of other people's thinking. Don't let the noise of others' opinions drown out your own inner voice. And most important, have the courage to follow your heart and intuition.

—STEVE JOBS

Follow your heart, but be quiet for awhile first. Ask questions and then feel the answer. Learn to trust your heart.

—UNKNOWN

In a conflict between the heart and brain, follow your heart.

—SWAMI VIVEKANANDA

Love the life you live. Live the life you love.

—BOB MARLEY

Your vision will become clear only when you look into your heart. Who looks outside, dreams; who looks inside, awakens.

—CARL JUNG

You can choose to follow your heart always.

—DON MIGUEL RUIZ

Go to your bosom: Knock there, and ask you heart what it doth know.

—WILLIAM SHAKESPEARE

Passion is a feeling that tell you: this is the right thing to do. Nothing can stand in my way. It doesn't matter what anyone else says. This feeling is so good that it cannot be ignored. I'm going to follow my bliss and act upon this glorious sensation of joy.

—Wayne Dyer

The best and most beautiful things in the world cannot be seen or even touched—they must be felt with the heart.

—Helen Keller

Forget about the fast lane. If you really want to fly, harness your power to your passion. Honor your calling. Everybody has one. Trust your heart, and success will come to you.

—Oprah Winfrey

Reflection

One of my favorite things to do living in Florida is to escape to the beach on the weekends to relax and reflect. This past weekend, I went a little earlier than I usually do. The weather was absolutely beautiful, so I decided to take a walk along the beach. The sun was beginning to rise; I could literally feel the beginning of a new day. The smell of the ocean breeze, the sound of the waves crashing, and the undeniable beauty that surrounded me, made me feel so alive. I started to reminisce of the past decade of my life. In this time of reflection, I began to gain extreme clarity. Everything started to become crystal clear to me. As I walked forward towards the sunrise, I realized that everything in my life thus far has had a specific purpose. Each decision, both good and bad, my relationships, jobs, career path, and even my healing journey were all part of God's plan for my life. Collectively, they worked together to bring me to where I am standing today.

We all are on our own unique journeys in this life. "Love Vision" has been my guide. Throughout my personal journey, I wasn't always able to see clearly due to the vision loss that I experienced from my surgery complication. Although, "Love Vision" gave me the strength and courage to view my world from another perspective. It ignited in me a passion to set out on a healing journey. It allowed me to open the eyes of my heart, and to live from a place of love. It gave me the freedom to live and to let go of fear. It taught me how to be a "Love Visionary," and to live my life with perseverance and passion. I learned the importance of building a vision for my life that would allow me to fulfill my purpose. At the same time, I also learned that things don't always happen overnight and that we don't always get exactly what it is that we desire. Sometimes what we want isn't what we truly need in our lives. I learned that I must live fully present in my own life. In learning how to walk by faith, I was divinely guided one step at a time.

LIVE A LIFE YOU LOVE

The first and most important decision that I made in my life when I discovered "Love Vision" was that I decided to commit to loving myself every day. This included taking care of myself and connecting with my mind, body, and soul on a daily basis, no matter what. In doing this, I was able to find healing and restoration. For when we truly learn how to unconditionally love ourselves, we are given the gift of "Love Vision" that forever changes the way in which we view ourselves, others, and the world. So, right now…my dear "Love Visionary"…I'm going to ask you to make the most important decision of your life in which you will commit to unconditionally love yourself. I challenge you to nurture your mind, body, and soul on a daily basis. Are you ready to live a life of "Love Vision"? Say yes to love. The decision will change you and your life forever.

"Love Vision" has given me the gift of living a life that I love, by allowing me to step into my authentic self and to live a life of freedom. My health, personal life, career, relationships, goals, desires, and dreams have all been affected by "Love Vision." I believe that everything in this world is interconnected and that love is the force that unites us all. Thank you for opening your heart and mind to "Love Vision." I hope that you have been enlightened to discover that you are the creator of your own life and that you're called for a higher purpose and destiny. Do not let your past define you. The past is in the past. The past is over and will never return. Your present and future life is waiting for you in this moment.

"Love Vision" has deeply inspired me to live my VISION through creating my dream company, "Love Vision," which is a life-coaching company dedicated to helping people create VISIONS that are built upon their purposes and passions so that they can live a life that they absolutely love! Through individual and group coaching, motivational speaking, and women's events, I'm blessed with the opportunity to be able to help others achieve their dreams. Let "Love Vision" inspire you to build your VISION so that you can live your purpose and passion. I am honored to call you my dear friend and a "Love Visionary"! It's time to get your "Love Vision" ON and start living a life you LOVE! You're destined to live your true passion and purpose. You have a legacy to fulfill. So, I would like to ask you one more question…..

Tell me, what is it you plan to do with your one wild and precious life?

—MARY OLIVER

The "Love Vision" Invitation

My dear "Love Visionary," as you venture into the beginning of your new journey, let us unite together to awaken a "Love Vision" generation! May we unconditionally love, serve, and support one another. Rise up and take a stand for love! Refuse to be silent. Our voices will be heard and our actions will ignite change. Miracles will manifest. Hope, peace, and freedom will touch the lives of many. Love will conquer.

#lovevision

The Beginning of Your "Love Vision" Journey

Resource Guide

My dear "Love Visionary," I'm honored to share with you some of the greatest resources that I have discovered along my "Love Vision" journey. These spiritual, motivational, and wellness experts have provided me with tremendous guidance, wisdom, and strength. My hope is that their teachings will bring more peace, balance, love, fulfillment, freedom, and faith into your life. As a Student of Love, let your heart be open to receive.

Spiritual Teachers

Heather Lee Beasley (lovevision.co): Check out the "LOVE VISION" website to sign up for our free weekly motivational e-newsletters and to learn more about the "LOVE VISION" membership, coaching services, online courses, and special events.

Dr. Deepak Chopra (deepakchopra.com): Words can't express how grateful I am for finding this amazing spiritual teacher over a decade ago. His work will change your life! Deepak Chopra is a *New York Times* best-selling author, meditation-guru, international speaker, alternative-medicine advocate, and spiritual activist. He is best known for his books *The Seven Spiritual Laws of Success*; *Ageless Body, Timeless Mind*; and *Perfect Health: The Complete Mind/Body Guide*.

Davidji (davidji.com): You're going to love Davidji! He is an internationally recognized stress-management expert, meditation teacher, and author of the best-selling books *destressifying: The Real-World Guide to Personal Empowerment, Lasting Fulfillment,* *and Peace of Mind* and *Secrets of Meditation: A Practical Guide to Inner Peace and Personal Transformation.*

Louise Hay (louisehay.com): Louise Hay has deeply inspired me to write *Love Vision.* She is known worldwide as one of the leading founders of the self-help movement and positive affirmations. She started Hay House Publishing, which is now one of the most successful mind-body-spirit publishing companies in the world. She is most known for her book *You Can Heal Your Life.*

Cheryl Richardson (cherylrichardson.com): Cheryl is a *New York Times* best-selling author and world-renowned life coach. She is most known for her books *Take Time for Your Life, The Art of Extreme Self Care, Life Makeovers* and *Stand Up for Your Life.*

Rhonda Byrne (thesecret.tv): Rhonda Byrne's book *The Secret* is a must read for every "Love Visionary." She teaches the life-changing principle that you must be willing to ASK, BELIEVE, and RECEIVE from the Universe. If you haven't yet read *The Secret,* you should definitely check it out! You will be inspired.

Nick Ortner (thetappingsolution.com): Nick Ortner is the *New York Times* best-selling author of *The Tapping Solution* and CEO of the Tapping Solution, LLC, a company dedicated to bringing a simple, effective, and natural healing into today's world through EFT (Emotional Freedom Technique), also known as "TAPPING."

Masting Kipp (thedailylove.com): This guy is genuine, real, and super inspirational! You can sign up on his website to receive free weekly emails and trainings. He is best known for his best seller, *Growing into Grace.* The book is beautiful!

Dr. Wayne Dyer (drwaynedyer.com): One of the pioneering leaders in self-help and spirituality, Wayne Dyer has written over forty books, including twenty *New York Times* best sellers, including *Change Your Thoughts—Change Your Life*, *The Power of Intention*, and *Your Erroneous Zones*. His legacy is destined to touch the lives of many.

Marrianne Williamson (marianne.com): She's one of the leading female spiritual teachers, authors, and lecturers. Marrianne is a *New York Times* best-selling author and is most known for her books *A Return to Love*, *A Woman's Worth*, and *A Course in Miracles*.

Gabby Bernstein (gabbybernstein.com): Gabby is an international speaker, self-proclaimed "Spirit Junkie," and *New York Times* best-selling author. She is most known for her books: *Spirit Junkie: A Road to Self-Love and Miracles*, *Miracles Now*, and *The Universe Has Your Back*.

Doreen Virtue (angeltherapy.com): If you're interested in learning more about your angels, you definitely will want to visit this website! Doreen Virtue is the founder of Angel Therapy and has written over fifty books on the subject of angels. She is an angel expert!

Motivational Teachers

Tony Robbins (tonyrobbins.com): Tony Robbins is the world's leading life success coach who is dedicated to helping people achieve their dreams. He is a *New York Times* best-selling author and is best known for his books *Awaken the Giant Within* and *Unlimited Power* and for his documentary, *Tony Robbins: I Am Not Your Guru.* Tony helps ignite your inner fire so that you can start taking unprecedented action toward manifesting your goals.

Brendon Burchard (brendon.com): Brendon Burchard is one of the most-watched and quoted personal development trainers in the world. Check out his website for insights on motivation, success, and tips on how to live a fully charged life!

Marie Forleo (marieforleo.com): Marie Forleo has been named by Oprah Winfrey as a thought leader of the next generation. She is the host of the award-winning online show *MarieTV* and is a founder of the Marie Forleo International and B-School. She's full of inspiration and words of wisdom to help you succeed both in your business and personal life.

Jonathon Fields (goodlifeproject.com): Jonathon Fields is the founder of the *Good Life Project.* His mission is to unite people together so that we can each help one another live more meaningful, connected, and fun lives.

John Assaraf (johnassaraf.com): John Assaraf is one of the world's leading behavioral and mind-set experts, who specializes in helping people release the mental and emotional obstacles that are preventing them from achieving success. He is the CEO of NeuroGym and a *New York Times* best-selling author most known for his books *Having It All: Achieving Your Life's Goals and Dreams* and *The Answer: Your Guide to Achieving Financial Freedom and Living an Extraordinary Life.*

Oprah Winfrey (Oprah.com): Opray Winfrey is America's most-loved talk show host. She has deeply inspired the lives of many with her courage, generosity, and motivation. Visit her website to stay up-to-date on her show, book club, the Angel Network, and her philanthropy work with Habitat for Humanity.

Wellness Teachers

MIND, BODY, GREEN (mindbodygreen.com): This is a healthy lifestyle website that is dedicated to revitalizing the way people eat, move, and live! I absolutely love this website and highly recommend that you check it out and sign up for their free healthy newsletters. This is totally worth it! They also offer a variety of online courses on all subjects: mind, body, and soul.

Dr. Christiane Northrup (drnorthrup.com): This is a doctor who truly understands women! She's wicked smart, witty, and full of wisdom! Check out her *New York Times* best sellers: *Goddesses Never Age, Women's Bodies, Women's Wisdom: Creating Physical and Emotional Health and Healing,* and *Beautiful Girl: Celebrating the Wonders of Your Body.*

Dr. Oz (doctoroz.com): Dr. Oz is America's most loved physician and host of the *Dr. Oz Show,* a daily television program focused on medical issues and personal health.

Kris Carr (kriscarr.com): Kris is a *New York Times* best-selling author, wellness activist, and cancer survivor. She's best known for her books *Crazy Sexy Cancer Survivor, Crazy Sexy Cancer Tips,* and a number of other awesome health-related books.

Lauren Scruggs Kennedy (laurenscruggskennedy.com): Lauren is a Wellness Warrior and a best-selling author and blogger. The goal of her blog is to teach people how to live a lifestyle that is rooted in balance. Lauren is an incredibly inspirational woman! She survived a plane-propeller accident that nearly took her life and resulted in the loss of her left hand and eye. But she didn't let that stop her from living her life to the fullest! Lauren and her husband have founded the Lauren Scruggs Kennedy Foundation, dedicated to bringing hope, restored dignity, and faith to girls and women with lost limbs, by providing them with beautiful cosmetic covering for prostheses. Visit lskfoundation.

com to learn more about how you can drastically help change the lives of women like Lauren. Check out her best-selling books: *Still Lo Lo* and *Your Beautiful Heart*.

Yoga Teachers

Tara Stiles (tarastiles.com): Tara Stiles is the founder of Strala Yoga, which is a revolutionary approach to achieve healing through movement. She was my first yoga instructor. Her studio is in NYC, so since I live in Florida, I have depended upon her DVDs and YouTube videos. She's authored numerous best sellers, including *Slim Calm Sexy Yoga, Yoga Cures, Make Your Own Rules Diet,* and *Make Your Own Rules Cookbook.* If you're searching for a yoga teacher, she's your girl!!

Hilaria Baldwin (livingclearlymethod.com): Hilaria Baldwin is a fitness and wellness expert, as well as the cofounder of Yoga Vida in NYC. She is the wife of Alec Baldwin, mother of three, business owner, yoga teacher, and author of the best-seller, *The Living Clearly Method.* Pick up a copy of her book, and she will teach you the five key principles that will help you maintain a fit body, healthy mind, and joyful life.

Kristin McGee (kristinmcgee.com): Kristin McGee is an eminent celebrity yoga and Pilates instructor. She is a trusted wellness expert, author, speaker, and "mompreneur." Kristin is dedicated to a teaching style that is fun and accessible. She's known for her popular yoga and Pilates DVDs that offer you the convenience to do yoga literally anytime and anywhere.

Bibliography

Mayo Clinic Staff. 2014. "Post-traumatic stress disorder (PTSD)." Last modified, April 15, 2014. http://www.mayoclinic.org/diseases-conditions/post-traumatic-stress-disorder/basics/definition/con-20022540.

Manish K Singh, MD. 2017. "Chronic Pain Syndrome." Medscape. Last modified January 24, 2017. http://www.emedicine.medscape.com/article/310834-overview.

Merriam Webster, s.v. "adaptation," February 8, 2017. https://www.merriam-webster.com/dictionary/adaptation.

Merriam Webster, s.v. "commitment," February 10, 2017. http://www.learnersdictionary.com/definition/commitment.

Merriam Webster, s.v. "rule," February 8, 2017. https://www.merriam-webster.com/dictionary/rule.

Merriam Webster, s.v. "rule," February 8, 2017. https://www.merriam- webster.com/dictionary/student.

Wikipedia, s.v. "puzzle," February 10, 2017. https://en.wikipedia.org/wiki/Puzzle.

Merriam Webster, s.v. "key," February 8, 2017. https://www.merriam- webster.com/dictionary/key.

Merriam Webster, s.v. "road map," February 8, 2017. https://www.merriam-webster.com/dictionary/road%20map.

Wikipedia. s.v. "creative visualization," February 8, 2017. https://en.wikipedia.org/ wiki/ Creative_visualization.

Dictionary.com, s.v. "emotion," February 8, 2017. http://www.dictionary.com/ browse/ emotion.

Merriam Webster, s.v. "emotion," February 8, 2017. https://www.merriam-webster.com/ dictionary/emotion.

Merriam Webster, s.v. "mantra," February 10, 2017. https://www.merriam-webster.com/ dictionary/mantra.

Merriam Webster, "heart," February 8, 2017. https://www.merriam-webster.com/ dictionary/heart.

Acknowledgments

God,

Thank you for being the source of all LOVE. Thank you for your grace, hope, and strength as we live our lives. Thank you for giving us the gift of "Love Vision" so that we may daily love ourselves, others, and the world around us. May our hearts be open to receiving your infinite love.

A Heartfelt Thank-You

I would like to express my deepest gratitude to the following spiritual teachers and successful leaders: Deepak Chopra, Louise Hay, Cheryl Richardson, Davidji, Mastin Kipp, Kris Carr, Gabrielle Bernstein, Dr. Christiane Northrup, Dr. Wayne Dyer, Marianne Williamson, John Assaraf, Oprah Winfrey, and Tony Robbins. From the bottom of my heart, thank you. Your teachings have deeply inspired me to share my message of "Love Vision" with the world. Thank you for sharing your authentic truth and messages of love, light, and hope. Your words inspired me in my darkest moments and gave me the courage to overcome my fears, pain, and inner demons in order to choose to live a life of love and freedom. It is on my "bucket list" to meet you all one day soon so that I can say thank you.

Rhonda Beasley: Thank you for being my best friend, mother, and spiritual inspiration. You have the biggest heart! You know how to love, nurture, care, support, and help others in a way that is extremely rare. Thank you for teaching me to have faith no matter what and to continue to believe that God has an awesome plan and purpose for my life! I will always love you with all of my heart.

Heidi Beasley: You will always be my little sister, Heidi Leigh! You're one of the most creative and talented people I've ever known. Keep creating and performing; your dreams will come true. No matter what, you will always be my favorite star!

Dad: I will always love you.

Tammy: I'm so glad that God placed you in my life. Your friendship has been such a blessing!

Joy, Jenny, Lizzie, and MeMe: You girls will always remain my favorite *Sex and the City* crew that I met upon moving to Florida during the most difficult time of my life. Your friendships, generosity, and love changed the course of my life. Thank you for becoming my "Florida family." I will never forget the memories, laughs, crazy times, and challenges that we all experienced together.

Gumma: To my "Gumma" in heaven…Thank you for teaching me how to be a "Love Visionary," spiritual warrior, and passionista! Your childlike spirit has taught me to never stop believing, creating, and—best of all—being my silly self. Your authenticity made you the most remarkable woman I've ever known. Thank you for your love, wisdom, and guidance.

Grandpa Beasley: Grandpa Beaz…Thank you for being my angel. I miss you. Thank you for always showing me love. I miss your big bear hugs. Thank you for teaching me what it means to be a leader and to help others. Thank you for helping me buy my first Honda Civic that enabled me to move to sunny South Florida! Thank you for always believing in me. Your entrepreneurial "Beaz" spirit lives on! I love you.

Grandma Beasley: "Wonder Woman" Beasley, you have truly taught me what it is to be a modern-day Wonder Woman! I will always be in awe of your superhuman powers to do it all, while successfully raising the "Biggest Beasley Broad" in the Burgh! Your legacy continues to live on. I love you.

Cassie Rockinson: I love you girl! Even though we live far apart, we'll always be close at heart. Thank you for your inspiration and encouragement. Your love and friendship mean so much to me. I'm so proud of you! You're an amazing mother!

Lauren Kennedy Scruggs: Lauren, from the bottom of my heart, I can't even begin to tell you how your faith has inspired me! Your personal story that you share in your book *Still Lo Lo* about your near-death plane propeller accident and your healing journey has provided me with a tremendous amount of encouragement, hope, and the strength to not give up on my healing journey. You're beautiful, brave, and bold! Your message has deeply affected my life.

The Author

Heather Lee Beasley is a certified life coach through the World Coach Institute. She is the founder of LOVE VISION, a life coaching company dedicated to helping people create VISIONS built upon their passions and purpose. Over the past eight years, Beasley has been successfully coaching private clients, women's groups, and hosting special events throughout Florida. Through the life-changing experience of almost permanently losing her vision, she was able to transform her personal tragedy into a passion for helping others to truly connect with their minds, bodies, and souls in order to find healing.

Heather was born and raised in Pittsburgh, Pennsylvania, and moved to sunny South Florida over a decade ago to pursue her passion and build a life that she loves. She is most passionate about her company LOVE VISION and helping people to live lives that they absolutely love! Her passion list includes motivational speaking and sharing the message of "Love Vision," writing, meditating, working out, practicing yoga, relaxing at the beach, enjoying the beautiful Florida sunsets, and spending time with her friends and family.

Her intimate and upbeat writing style, powerful questioning, and self-development exercises will take you on a "Love Vision" journey of self-discovery that will enable you to gain clarity on your goals, values, dreams, and VISION so that you can begin taking immediate action in order to live your best life now. To learn more about LOVE VISION, visit www.lovevision.co

www.ingramcontent.com/pod-product-compliance
Lightning Source LLC
Chambersburg PA
CBHW062037090426
42740CB00016B/2932

9 780692 838297